P R A I S E   F O R

Praying Through Your Child's
Early Years

Laying a foundation for your child in understanding prayer, worship, a fasted lifestyle and serving is critical. I love how Jennifer and Carolyn walk with you, day by day and step by step, through your child's most important needs during his or her first five years. *Praying Through Your Child's Early Years* is a comprehensive guide in teaching your child these valuable principles.

Katy Cerney
Ministry Leader, International House of Prayer

Praying Through Your Child's Early Years recognizes the demanding nature of motherhood. As moms, we are often so busy meeting the needs of those around us that we forget to take care of ourselves. Jennifer uses her personal experience and professional training to offer practical, realistic ways for new moms to care for their physical, emotional and spiritual needs. Although it takes time, and sometimes feels selfish, taking care of ourselves helps us to be better moms for our kids.

Alexandra Kuykendall
Content Editor, MOPS International
Author of *The Artist's Daughter*

An Inspirational Year-by-Year Guide for
Raising a Spiritually Healthy Child

Praying Through Your Child's
Early Years

Jennifer Polimino
& Carolyn Warren

Authors of *Praying Through Your Pregnancy*

Regal

For more information and
special offers from Regal Books, email us at
subscribe@regalbooks.com

Published by Regal
From Gospel Light
Ventura, California, U.S.A.
www.regalbooks.com
Printed in the U.S.A.

Library of Congress Cataloging-in-Publication Data
Polimino, Jennifer.
Praying through your child's early years : an inspirational year-by-year guide
for raising a spiritually healthy child / Jennifer Polimino, Carolyn Warren.
p. cm.
Includes bibliographical references and index.
ISBN 978-0-8307-6389-4 (hard cover : alk. paper)
1. Parents—Religious life. 2. Parents—Prayers and devotions. 3. Parenting—
Religious aspects—Christianity. 4. Child rearing—Religious aspects–Christianity.
I. Warren, Carolyn. II. Title.
BV283.C5P65 2012
248.8'45—dc23
2012023361

Rights for publishing this book outside the U.S.A. or in non-English languages are
administered by Gospel Light Worldwide, an international not-for-profit ministry.
For additional information, please visit www.glww.org, email info@glww.org, or write
to Gospel Light Worldwide, 1957 Eastman Avenue, Ventura, CA 93003, U.S.A.

To order copies of this book and other Regal products in bulk quantities,
please contact us at 1-800-446-7735.

Dedication

We dedicate this book to our mothers,
Sharon Stimac and Barbara Barnett Lockhart,
who taught us the value and power of prayer
through their own lives.

Contents

Part III: Your Baby Is All Grown Up

AGES FOUR TO FIVE

Prologue

Your Baby Enters the World

In case you missed our first book, *Praying Through Your Pregnancy*, this prologue will catch you up on what we wrote there. In this book you'll get to know me, Jennifer Polimino, now mother to Micah and Malia Grace. Later in the book, you'll also hear from my husband, Dan, and from coauthor Carolyn Warren, mom of two grown children and grandmother to six grandchildren (one adopted from Ethiopia).

Each chapter begins with an excerpt from my personal journal and ends with a Parent's Prayer, Scriptures for Thought and Meditation, and a place for you to jot down your own thoughts as a special keepsake and blessing to share with your son or daughter in the future.

Jennifer's Journal

I kept my calendar open this week for the baby to come. My due date was on Monday, and now it's Friday. Still, there's no sign of the baby. What's going on? I feel like I'm going to be pregnant FOREVER. I'm in week 42.

He was supposed to be here on July 25 or sooner, according to the doctors. I keep walking on the trails behind my house, trying to help this baby along. I tried some completely safe, natural remedies that people swear by, like eating spicy foods, but all that did was make my tummy upset.

I called Betty, my massage therapist, to come over and try to help this baby along, too, but that didn't work either. It did enable me to relax

> *though, and Betty assured me that the baby would be here in God's time,*
> *not ours. I know she's right. Every pregnancy is different, every labor is*
> *different and every birth is different. God knows what He is doing.*

My due date was July 25, 2005, but the day came and went with no baby. The same thing happened the next day and the next, until the calendar turned to August. When strangers asked me when my baby was due, they looked concerned. I was so ready to meet my son.

August 1 came and went, and nothing happened. August 2 came and went, and nothing happened. And then, finally, on the afternoon of August 3, my contractions began—and continued the rest of the day and all night.

Squatting seemed to be the best position for me, but after 24 hours of squatting, and handling contractions, I was exhausted. It was now August 4, nine days after the due date. Fortunately, I was able to sleep for a few hours when the contractions subsided.

At four o'clock the next afternoon, I called Janet, my doula, to let her know. My husband, Dan, was extremely comforting; he wanted to do whatever he could to help. But I was pretty much handling the contractions on my own and wanted him to get his sleep. I figured I'd really need him later.

I think it was about 3:00 A.M. when I called Janet again, and God bless her for coming over in the middle of the night. Dan was much more interested in heading for the hospital than either Janet or I. We convinced him to go back to sleep, promising to call the doctor's office in the morning. I didn't want to go to the hospital just to be sent home again, since it was so far away—a good 30- to 40-minute drive each way.

When I called the doctor's office, they said I couldn't *possibly* be in labor because I was interested in brushing my teeth and drying my hair. (I had been in the tub half the night, dealing with contractions.) Nevertheless, we set an appointment, and off Janet and I went at about 8:30 A.M. We convinced Dan to head out to work, with a promise to call him if anything changed substantially. After all, this had been going on pretty much for two days already.

Emmy, my nurse, said, "You're dilated three to four centimeters."

I thought that was fantastic news. I said, "Praise God! At least these contractions are *doing* something."

Emmy said, "I want you to check into the hospital by noon."

But I had a different idea. I was starving, so we all ate lunch together back at home—with me standing up to lean forward or to squat during every contraction, and Dan praying for God's help and strength. We then set off for the hospital to get there by two o'clock.

I did *not* enjoy the trip to the hospital; but then again, it wasn't as bad as I'd expected. The contractions were actually not as strong in the car—maybe it was the movement or the change of scenery.

I sat in the back seat per Janet's suggestion. Whenever a contraction came, I put one leg up on the seat, the other on the floor and held on to the baby's car seat. I must have been *quite* a sight, and I remember wanting to wave at the people driving by who were gawking at me.

We arrived at St. Joseph's Hospital in downtown Denver, and I hoisted myself out of the car. My water bag immediately broke all over the parking lot. (Dan was so happy it didn't happen in the car!) However, when we got up to the maternity ward, they made the decision that my water bag had *not* broken. Imagine that! Obviously, they had not been in the parking lot when it happened.

I refused to let them check my cervix. I didn't want to risk introducing an infection since I *knew* my water bag had broken—even though they couldn't get any of their tests to verify it.

I continued to squat through every contraction. Dan kept giving me water to drink or ice chips to munch on, and he played Hawaiian music to soothe me. Over and over, I begged him to not fall asleep. I needed him *now!* One thing about my husband is that he can sleep anywhere, *anytime*. Nonetheless, he promised he wouldn't—and he didn't.

I remember sitting on the birth ball for part of the time, but mostly it's kind of a blur. I know this much: It was difficult. I also remember pushing for about an hour. I was really feeling out of it at that point since I'd hardly slept in three days and had been in labor for over 30 hours with no medication whatsoever. And I can't lie—it hurt.

Then, at exactly 9:28 P.M., on August 5, 2005, my beautiful baby boy, Micah Kekoa Polimino, was born. Praise the Lord! God is so good.

I could never have imagined the overwhelming love I would experience for this child. This was my own little boy, a part of me. I would do anything to protect him. I love him more than I love my own life. And then the realization hit me. This is how God feels about us. It's amazing to think that God sent His own beloved Son, Jesus, to die for us on the cross so that we might be with Him in heaven. How could He make such a colossal sacrifice for us? I certainly didn't feel worthy; but experiencing the love I have for my own little boy, I finally got it. God did what was necessary to save us from evil.

When your baby enters the world and you hold him or her in your arms, you understand what I'm talking about. This child is truly a gift from God. We women are so blessed to experience this miracle of childbirth. It's not easy, but it is truly amazing.

I can't help but think about how Mary must have felt when she first held Jesus in her arms. She had just gone through nine months of ridicule and rejection. Her friends had disowned her, and she was newly married to Joseph, who thought she'd been unfaithful, before the angel's visitation set him straight. When she was ready to deliver, she had to travel to Bethlehem to pay taxes, riding on a donkey over unpaved, possibly rock-filled and pot-holed roads, for three days; and now she had just given birth to the Son of God . . . in a stable. She had every reason to question God, but instead she praised Him.

As she held her new baby—the Messiah—in her arms, I can only imagine the love and joy she must have felt. Her smile must have reached all the way to the depths of her soul.

My son, Micah, brought a smile to my face too; the waiting was finally over. It was a long three days, but my baby was here!

I hope your child's birth was much less traumatic than mine. I pray that when your little one arrived, he or she was perfect, and you got to enjoy those first few days in feelings of awe and wonder, and you experienced growing closer to God than ever before. I hope you discovered a new sense of meaning in your life.

My baby's birth changed my life forever, and I pray that wonderful change for you as well.

Parent's Prayer

Dear Father God,

Words cannot express the joy I have right now that my baby is finally here. Thank You for this most precious gift, for this precious life. Please help me, Lord, to love this baby like You do. Help me to be the parent You desire me to be. Help me to teach this baby about You, Jesus. Please provide for, protect and encourage my little one.

Pour into my baby's heart Your joy, peace and love, and watch over him/her these first few weeks. Show me the right things to do, and give me strength and sleep when I need it most. Help me to teach my baby the true meaning of Your agape love—to love unconditionally. As I hold [put your baby's name here], let him/her feel Your love, Father. Thank You, Jesus.

In Your mighty name I pray, amen.

Scriptures for Thought and Meditation

Sing to the Lord with thanksgiving; sing praises on the harp to our God.
PSALM 147:7

And you will have joy and gladness, and many will rejoice at his birth.
LUKE 1:14

My Journal

Keeping a journal will help create a special bond with your child and also hold profound meaning for him or her someday. You can use the space at the end of each chapter to describe the birth and growth of your child.

PART I

Your Child's First Year

Give thanks to the Lord of lords!
His love is eternal.

PSALM 136:3, CSB

1

Baby's First Weeks

Jennifer's Journal

My Micah has finally arrived! It feels like I've been waiting for years for him to join our family, and now he's finally here. But something's not right. He's not crying like newborn babies do. The nurses began to get worried, and I could see they thought something was wrong. "Lord, what is wrong with him? Please make him all right . . . please, Jesus," I prayed over and over again.

The doctors quickly informed my husband and me that the cord had been wrapped around his neck—not once, but twice—and he must have aspirated on the way out.

"He needs to go to the NICU right away. He has streaking in his lungs," the doctor said. "He has to have some tests done, antibiotics delivered, and oxygen administered."

The medical staff rushed him out of my room and into NICU. "Stay with him, don't let him out of your sight!" I yelled to my husband as he ran out the door after our sweet baby.

"Why, God?" I cried quietly to myself. "Why would You put me through this only to take away my firstborn son?"

The situation at the hospital seemed like a disaster. First, I like to be in control of my situation, so it's hard for me to have someone else telling me what to do. And next, I feel strongly about not putting unnecessary drugs and chemicals into my body, let alone into my newborn baby's body. As a health and nutrition coach and personal trainer for the past 20 years, I love teaching people how to live a healthy, natural lifestyle. I had just finished two long, grueling days of all-natural childbirth to avoid having drugs go into my baby, and now to have the doctors tell me they needed to give my newborn antibiotics and other drugs—well, let's just say this didn't sit well with me.

During the next four days, I hardly left Micah's side. I sat holding him in the NICU (Neonatal Intensive Care Unit) while they poked, prodded and tested him. Dan said he had to go back to work, but I think he just couldn't bear to sit there and wait for the results to come back. The doctors conducted test after test and convinced Dan that Micah needed a spinal tap. I fought against that, but in the end, Dan said we had no choice. During this painful procedure, Micah never cried a single tear. I did that for him. The nurses kept telling me to go back to my room and get some sleep, but I just couldn't leave my baby. What if he needed me? What if he wanted to nurse? What if he pooped? I wanted to be the one to take care of him, feed him and change his tiny diaper!

Day after day, and night after night, I listened to the nurses tell me stories about the other babies in the NICU. Some circumstances were simply heart-wrenching. One little guy, in a crib right next to Micah's, caught my attention. I had seen his dad come in only one time during the four days I sat and rocked Micah. That sweet baby was born a preemie but was now about six months old. All of the nurses were like mothers to him. Every time they switched shifts, the new nurse on duty immediately picked him up and proceeded to talk to him and love him.

God provided this little guy with angels to watch over him and take care of him while his parents were unable to be there. I later learned this family lived far away from the hospital. The father had to go back to work to pay the medical bills, and the mom had to be at home to take care of her other kids. I'm sure it broke her heart to know she couldn't hold her new baby each night. She had no choice but to put her trust in the nurses—women she didn't even know.

I've always had an issue with trusting people in my life, so releasing my baby into God's hands was very difficult for me in the beginning. But it has been something I've had to do time and time again. From the first time I left Micah with a sitter to his first day at school, I learned to trust God to protect and watch over my baby; and I pray you will be able to do that with your child as well.

Daddy's Blog

I was sitting in a room full of soon-to-be dads on a Saturday morning in July, at St. Joseph's hospital. The class started at 8:00 A.M., and Jennifer thought it would be a good idea for me to learn a few things about newborns. It's called the "Daddy Boot Camp." I am all for being prepared, but on a Saturday morning at eight o'clock in the middle of summer . . . *talking about diapers?* I was less than enthusiastic.

They say if you can remember one important point from a class or seminar, you have done okay. The guy teaching the class said at the very beginning, "*Expect the unexpected.*" That was the one thing I remembered. He went on to say that everyone plans, everyone has an idea of how the birth is going to go and everyone has his or her own expectations. He told us to throw them out the window, because in most cases it never goes to plan. That terrified me, which is why I probably remembered that one point. You see, I am a type-A personality. I plan everything! Yes, our birth was going to go just like we planned. I was going to make sure of it.

Micah came out with the umbilical cord wrapped twice around his neck. He wasn't breathing well, and he had fluid in his lungs. I could tell by the look on the faces of the nurses and doctors that something was wrong. They told us he needed to go to NICU right away, and suddenly it felt like someone had just hit me over the head with a sledgehammer. Things were moving so fast, and I was trying to regain some control. As I followed the doctors who had my baby boy, I was thinking, *What about Jen? What are they doing to my son? What's wrong with him? Is he going to be okay? The unexpected has just happened, and now everything has changed.*

Releasing your child into someone else's hands, even if that someone is God, is probably one of the hardest things to do, especially as a first-time parent. I knew in my head that God wants us to give Him everything, including our children; but in my heart, this was very difficult to do. After all, this was my first child, and Micah was my *baby*.

On that very first day, I had to step back and give Micah to God, and trust Him. I had to hold on to Psalm 32:10: "Steadfast love surrounds the one who trusts in the LORD" (*ESV*). Even though I was the one who had just given birth to this sweet little boy, God reminded me that Micah was, first of all, His. God wanted me to know that He is always in control and will always be in control. He is the First and the Last, the Great I AM, the Lord of lords, the Beginning and the End.

When the Holy Spirit reminded me of Revelation 1:8, "'I am the Alpha and the Omega, the Beginning and the End,' says the Lord, 'who is and who was and who is to come, the Almighty,'" I knew I could not help but trust Him with my son.

If we can grasp this concept right from the very beginning and offer our children to God from day one, we will be richly blessed indeed. We will live a more peaceful and joyful lives free from fear. Jesus told us, "Peace I leave with you, My peace I give to you; not as the world gives do I give to you. Let not your hearts be troubled, neither let it be afraid" (John 14:27).

On Micah's fifth day, we were discharged from the hospital. They put me in a wheelchair—hospital rules—and wheeled me with our new baby and his little oxygen tank downstairs to our Nissan Murano. We were so happy to finally go home. Dan placed Micah in the back in his five-point harness car seat, and I sat right next to him—just in case he needed me.

I think Dan drove 20 miles per hour all the way home! We stopped at our favorite Middle Eastern restaurant, called Jerusalem, and Dan ran in and got Chicken Shawarma and a lamb shank to go. I was starving. I had hardly eaten in the last seven days, and I'd burned thousands of calories during labor. The hospital food wasn't great, but the main reason was that I never wanted to leave my baby's side. On the last day, they allowed Micah to come into my room and sleep by me, but I was never able to get any quality sleep there, with the nurses in and out of my room every hour. If it wasn't to check on Micah or me, it was to have me sign more paperwork.

Our Eclectus parrots, Lani and Logan, greeted us with loud screams when we walked in the front door. I've had my parrots for more than 16 years. Lani-girl flew with me on the plane from Hawaii in a little carrying case under the seat in front of me. Many people have dogs or cats as their "kids" prior to having children, but because of my allergies, we had birds.

I took Micah in my arms and kissed him gently. "This is your brother, Logan, and your big sister, Lani," I told him jokingly. The birds stared at Micah in amusement. They had no idea how their lives were going to change. And neither did I. "My little man," as I called him, completely changed my life forever.

For the first two weeks, it seemed like I never stopped praying that God would heal the streaking in Micah's lungs and make him completely healthy. He seemed perfectly fine to me, but his oxygen tank was a constant reminder that he wasn't 100 percent there yet, and God was the only one who could heal him. I'd grab the Moses basket Micah was lying in with one hand, and with the other, I'd carry the oxygen tank and take him with me wherever I went. The Apria healthcare nurses stopped by our home every day or two to check on Micah's oxygen tank and make sure he was doing fine.

When Micah was two weeks old, we decided to go to a different doctor, who told us, "Your baby is absolutely fine; he doesn't need oxygen anymore." *Thank You, Jesus!* Dan and I were absolutely thrilled.

Months earlier, I had planned on taking Micah to meet my parents in Hawaii when he was about five weeks old; but because he was born almost two weeks later than expected, our flight reservations meant that we were leaving less than a week after he got off of the oxygen. It had been iffy as to whether we could take the trip, but now we had permission, and I was thrilled!

The following week, Micah and I boarded a plane back to my hometown, Kailua-Kona, which is located on the Big Island of Hawaii. I was a bit nervous about flying with a newborn, but my mom assured me we would be fine. I had My Brest Friend blow-up pillow—which I consider a must-have if you travel with a nursing or lap child—a stroller, a camera and a huge diaper bag. The flight attendants were accommodating and helpful, and I was so fortunate the flight wasn't full. I was able to spread out in an empty row with Micah for the eight hours in the air.

I remember praying a lot during the flight. I was so worried his little ears would start hurting and I wouldn't get him to nurse. Thankfully, he did just fine. I only put him down once during those eight-plus hours, to use the restroom while the flight attendant held him. When the plane finally touched down, I descended the steep stairs onto the tarmac of our little Kona airport with my arms full. My parents were there to greet their newest grandchild, and it felt so good to be home in the warm, fresh Kona air. Despite my worries, God had truly taken care of each and every detail.

We spent two weeks visiting with family and enjoying time on the white sandy beaches where I grew up. I purchased a great little tent to protect Micah from the tropical sun, and he slept in it for hours. Dan even surprised us by flying in for four days. He said he couldn't stand being away from his son. He missed Micah so much that the two days of flying was worth it just to hold our baby again. Hearing Dan say that made me think that is how God feels about us.

Your heavenly Father longs to spend time with you. Right now, things may seem crazy-busy with a newborn; but I encourage you to seek the Lord each and every day. For me, the best time to commune with God was when I was nursing Micah. I sat and relaxed and read my Bible or prayed. I couldn't help but feel gratitude for how blessed I was. I used that quiet time to thank God for this most amazing gift, my baby.

No matter how seemingly insane your life feels right now with your inability to sleep through the night, hormonal adjustments messing with your emotions and learning to fit this new little person into your schedule, find a consistent time when you can talk to God and listen for His voice. Believe me, it makes all the difference.

My weeks were unusual with my little man on special oxygen. I hope your first weeks are better. In the coming chapters, we'll talk about many of the normal challenges a new baby creates and how to pray through them with confidence.

Parent's Prayer

Dear heavenly Father,

Thank You for my sweet baby. Lord, I give (child's name) to You. You are the King of kings and the Lord of lords, and I know You care about my baby. Mold me into the parent You want me to be. Help me to make the right decisions for her/him and follow You always.

Please help me when I have worries and doubts about what's going on. Help me to remain calm and stay centered in You. Give me Your peace that passes all understanding. Let me stand firm in the knowledge that You are the alpha and omega, the beginning and the end—the almighty God.

In every difficult circumstance, be my rock and fortress. In times of trouble, be my deliverer. Give me strength that is beyond my own, shield me from the Enemy.

Lord Jesus, I give thanks to You because You are a good God and Your mercy endures forever. Thank You so much for this precious baby You have given me. Watch over him/her today and always.

In Jesus' name, I pray, amen.

Scriptures for Thought and Meditation

"I am the Alpha and the Omega, the Beginning and the End," says the Lord, "who is and who was and who is to come, the Almighty."
REVELATION 1:8

Oh, give thanks to the Lord of lords! For His mercy endures forever.
PSALM 136:3

My Journal

What I want my child to know about who God is:

_____

_____

_____

_____

_____

_____

_____

_____

_____

_____

_____

_____
_____
_____
_____
_____
_____
_____
_____
_____
_____
_____
_____
_____

A special prayer for my baby:

_____
_____
_____
_____
_____
_____
_____
_____
_____
_____
_____
_____
_____
_____
_____
_____
_____

2

How to Be a Praying Parent

Jennifer's Journal

My little man warms my heart like never before. He is so sweet. I set up a mini photo shoot for him today in our home. I needed a picture for our birth announcement, and we can't afford a photographer, so I did it myself. I'm pretty good at taking pictures, and I sure do enjoy it. My husband says this little guy will have thousands of photos by the time he is a year old. I'm sure he's right! I just can't put the camera down; I know it's because I don't want to forget anything or miss anything, or miss any special moments.

I prayed a lot for Micah all through my pregnancy, and now that he's here, I pray that he will grow to become a man of God and never depart from Him, as I did in my teenage years and my twenties. That's why I've been asking God for guidance. I want to be a mother who is loving, compassionate and understanding. I know God hears and answers our prayers.

Last week at the Women of Faith conference, Amy Grant sang her song "Better Than a Hallelujah." That song describes my prayer life.

When we cry out to God and pour out our miseries to Him, God hears a melody. Even when we are a complete mess and our hearts are breaking, sometimes a desperate plea is better than singing a hallelujah, because we're being real. God wants to hear from us. Whatever we are concerned or worried about is what we need to tell Him. God is with us, waiting for us to talk to Him.

My prayer life *really* began when I found out I was pregnant with Micah. I had prayed in the past, but it was not with the same sense of urgency as when I found out we were finally expecting. While pregnant, I was worried and scared about so many different things, but I turned to God for His guidance and help.

After Micah was born, and the months flew by, I began to realize the prayers I prayed while pregnant were coming to pass. I was amazed that God heard and cared enough to answer my prayers! From the important to the insignificant, what mattered to me also mattered to Him. I am now very passionate about the power of prayer. Prayer brings God into your life, and I want that for you. I want you to experience the phenomenal power that comes from being a praying parent.

You become a praying parent as you go about your day. It's not about following a rigid routine or keeping track of time; it's about making prayer a natural part of your life. Prayer becomes a part of who you are. For example, I teach my children that no matter where we are, we will always give thanks in prayer for our blessings. I teach my kids to pray when we hear an ambulance or see someone in need.

Regardless of whether we're having a bad day or a great day, we take time out to talk to God. If we get a great parking spot or if we see a rainbow, we always say, "Thank You, Lord." At each meal, we thank our heavenly Father for providing for us. It's those little things that teach children that God is real. We treat God as we would treat a friend who is right there with us, all the time, and we talk to Him. It's like George Buttrick said, "Prayer is friendship with God."[1]

I was fortunate to grow up in a Christian home, so we prayed every day; but even if you did not grow up in a home with praying parents, you can create a legacy of prayer for your children. When you model the belief that prayer is essential and that prayer works, your children will adopt it as well.

I remember that my mom and dad prayed often, especially when the whole family was together for dinner around the big dining room table. Many times, we took turns thanking Jesus for our blessings. It was a time to connect with God and be unified as a family.

Now, as parents, my husband and I make a point of teaching our children to *believe* in prayer. Each time God answers a prayer, like helping my son do his best at his soccer game, or healing a sick family member or giving my husband a home sale in his real estate business, we thank Him for answering our prayers.

There is not a proper way to pray. Prayer is simply talking with God, and He is faithful to meet you wherever you are.

Prayer doesn't have to be poetic or profound. Matthew 12:25 tells us that Jesus knew the people's thoughts. We read in Psalm 139:2, "I'm an open book to you; even from a distance, you know what I'm thinking" (*THE MESSAGE*). If God knows our thoughts, then surely we can talk to Him like we're talking to our very best friend.

Nana's Journal

My grandson is a typical boy. At age two, his favorite things in the world are big trucks. He knows the difference between a logger, a loader, a backhoe, a digger, an excavator and all the other fascinating construction machines.

He likes spyglasses, Army men and Curious George.

He builds forts, roads and hideouts. If you have a grandson, I'm sure you're familiar with all of this.

One afternoon when I was baby-sitting, we were drawing pictures of rockets. Out of the blue, he looked at me and said, "The most important thing is God."

"Wow," I thought, "his Bible teaching is taking hold." We then had ourselves a short but meaningful discussion about God, and I went home feeling uplifted and blessed.

Carolyn Warren

Praying Is Also Listening

So often we forget to be quiet and listen for God's voice. Prayer is more than talking *to* God; it's also about listening for what He wants to say to us. When Jesus went to the Mount of Olives to commune with God, He went to hear from God as well as to speak to Him.

I remember hearing God speak to me about writing our first book, *Praying Through Your Pregnancy*. Micah was about two years old when I began to notice that many of the prayers I had prayed while pregnant were coming to pass. So I prayed about it, and God clearly told me He wanted me to write a book to inform mothers of the importance of praying for their unborn babies. I know without a doubt that writing that book (as well as this one) was His will.

Asking God for a Blessing

Scripture tells us, "Then they also brought infants to Him that He might touch them" (Luke 18:15). I love this scene where parents are bringing their precious newborn babies to Jesus to receive a blessing. There is no indication that any of the infants were ill; the parents simply wanted Jesus to touch their sons and daughters. We read that the disciples tried to protect Jesus from what they perceived as an intrusion. They figured that Jesus had more important business to attend to, such as the adults. The disciples actually scolded the parents and tried to shoo them away. I wonder how many of those parents were disappointed, ready to give up on their desire. Fortunately, the story doesn't end there. "But Jesus called them to Him and said, 'Let the little children come to Me, and do not forbid them; for of such is the kingdom of God'" (v. 16).

I love how Jesus demonstrated His love for babies. Let that strengthen your faith whenever you talk to the Lord about your child. Jesus loves your son and/or daughter, and He wants to touch them. As parents, we are to intercede for them when we pray: "Pour out your heart like water in the presence of the Lord. Lift up your hands to him for the lives of your children" (Lam. 2:19, *NIV*). It really is okay to bring Him every concern. The following Scriptures encourage us to pray for what we need:

Five Faith-Building Scriptures on Asking and Receiving

"And whatever things you ask in prayer, believing, you will receive" (Matt. 21:22).

"So I say to you, ask, and it will be given to you; seek, and you will find; knock, and it will be opened to you. For everyone who asks receives, and he who seeks finds, and to him who knocks, it will be opened" (Luke 11:9–10).

"And whatever you ask in My name, that I will do, that the Father may be glorified in the Son. And if you ask anything in My name, I will do it" (John 14:13–14).

"If you abide in Me, and My words abide in you, you will ask what you desire, and it shall be done for you" (John 15:7).

"Until now you have asked nothing in My name. Ask, and you will receive, that your joy may be full" (John 16:24).

Finding Time to Pray

It's common to feel too busy or too tired to set aside time to pray, and Jesus understands that feeling. But He is our model for the importance of consistently seeking God in prayer. He was pressed by the crowds to teach and to heal. On several occasions there was standing room only (see Luke 5:18-19). The needs of the people were never-ending, and yet, Jesus took time away from the demands of the ministry to walk to the top of a nearby mountain and spend time communing with His Father. If the Son of God prioritized spending time in prayer to become spiritually recharged and refreshed, how much more do we need to find time to pray?

As you read the upcoming chapters, I pray that you will be inspired to pray and that your faith will be strengthened. The adage "Prayer changes things" is true. Never underestimate the power of prayer; it has the power to spiritually change your child's life. Every prayer you pray for your child is a seed sown into his or her destiny.

How powerful is that! In Revelation 5:8, we read, "The Four Animals and Twenty-four Elders fell down and worshiped the Lamb. Each had a harp and each had a bowl, a gold bowl filled with incense, the prayers of God's holy people" (*THE MESSAGE*). God on His throne has our prayers right next to Him in a golden bowl. What a wonderful picture of how He values our prayers!

Parent's Prayer

Dear God,

Help me to be a praying mom/dad. Help me show my child, through the way I live, that prayer is important. Help me to be a good example each and every day. Let me not forget to express gratefulness for Your daily blessings.

Lord, increase my faith. When I am afraid or full of doubt, lift me up and strengthen me. Help me to claim the promises in Scripture as my own and tap into Your power through praying Your Word. You said to ask and then receive. I am asking You to give me faith to become a praying parent; and in faith, I receive it.

I ask You to bless my baby, [your child's name]. Bless her/him with a wonderful, happy life. Bless her/him with Your holy presence and love. Watch over and keep her/him from all harm. I pray that my child will learn to pray at a young age and grow to be a person of great faith.

In Jesus' name I pray, amen.

Scriptures for Thought and Meditation

Pour out your heart like water before the face of the Lord.
Lift your hands toward Him for the life of your young children.
LAMENTATIONS 2:19

Let us therefore come boldly to the throne of grace, that we may obtain mercy and find grace to help in time of need.
HEBREWS 4:16

My Journal

My journey to becoming a praying parent:

_____
_____
_____
_____
_____
_____
_____
_____
_____
_____
_____
_____
_____
_____
_____

I want to sow these prayer seeds into my child's destiny:

_____
_____
_____
_____
_____
_____
_____
_____
_____
_____
_____
_____
_____
_____

Note

1. Richard J. Foster and James Bryan Smith, *Devotional Classics: Selected Readings for Individuals and Groups* (New York: Harper Collins, 2005), p. 87.

3

Feeding and Bonding
with Your Baby

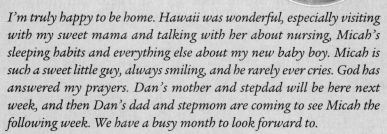

Jennifer's Journal

I'm truly happy to be home. Hawaii was wonderful, especially visiting with my sweet mama and talking with her about nursing, Micah's sleeping habits and everything else about my new baby boy. Micah is such a sweet little guy, always smiling, and he rarely ever cries. God has answered my prayers. Dan's mother and stepdad will be here next week, and then Dan's dad and stepmom are coming to see Micah the following week. We have a busy month to look forward to.

I hope this little guy will realize someday how many people love him. He has his mom and dad who think the world of him, three sets of grandparents, at least eight sets of aunts and uncles, tons of cousins and my 82-year-old grandma, who we call Candy Grandma, because she used to sneak candy to us when we were kids. I'm so excited that my grandma will be coming for a visit soon; I know she will just love Micah.

On another note, Micah has taken well to nursing, and I understand his hunger cues much better now. Those first days at the hospital were tough. In less than 12 hours after giving birth, the nurses wanted me to start pumping so that I could give Micah milk while he was in intensive care. They said if my milk didn't come in soon, they were going

> *to give him formula. I prayed and prayed for my milk to come in, and oh boy, did it ever! When I carried the little Ziploc bags into the NICU, the nurses couldn't believe how much milk I had already. It made me feel so happy. They called it "liquid gold." I know that God caused my milk to come in time as an answer to my prayers. He cares about every little detail that is important to me.*

Toward the end of my pregnancy, I did some serious thinking and read a lot of books about how I was going to feed my baby and what options I'd have. My desire was to nurse my baby, but I didn't know if I would be able to. You see, more than 14 years ago, I had been a fitness competitor, and I competed for years in the Fitness America and Galaxy competitions, as well as in state contests. To get that perfect body, I maintained a strenuous workout schedule doing cardio, strength and flexibility training for more than four hours a day. Fitness was my life at that time: self-centered and self-fulfilling. I was not walking with the Lord at that point in my life, and having a perfect body was on the top of my priority list.

I did very well and even won a few state competitions; nevertheless, the owner of a top fitness magazine told me if I wanted to win at the national level, I needed to get breast implants. I already had self-esteem issues due to being a victim of abuse in the past, and I had been thinking for a while that implants would help me feel better about myself. After receiving his suggestion, I went ahead and did it.

Having the procedure did not help at all; my self-esteem stayed the same. And now, many years later and pregnant with my first child, I greatly regretted my decision. This was a major concern to me, because I didn't know if I would be able to nurse Micah or not. Although I tried researching for answers, there really wasn't much information available on the subject. My doctor told me, "You'll just have to wait and see."

Not knowing what else to do, I decided to give my concern to God. During the last three months of my pregnancy, this was a daily topic in my prayers. I told my heavenly Father how badly I wanted to nurse my child, just like He created me to do, and I asked Him to make it a wonderful and bonding experience with my baby.

When Micah finally arrived, and I began to pump in the hospital and my milk came in, I was ecstatic! God had answered my prayers. My baby knew exactly what to do, and breastfeeding was a wonderful bonding experience for me. You might also be nursing your baby, or you might be bottle-feeding. Either way, I am here to encourage you and help you understand the benefits of bonding with your baby.

Daddy's Blog

Guys, I have to be honest here. When Jen's milk came in, all I could say was, WOW! This is going to be great. But she promptly informed me that those were not for my enjoyment anymore—or at least I was going to have restricted access. Micah took to nursing like a fish to water, rarely wanting to stop; and after feeding him all day, the last thing Jen wanted was me.

It took a little while to adjust to that, but when I saw how happy Micah was and how happy Jen was, I dealt with it. "I took one for team," as they say in sports. I think the toughest part was trying to figure out my role at this stage. Newborns are so dependent on their mamas and feeding that dads are left asking, *What am I supposed to do?* If you are bottle-feeding, dads can have a great role in feeding the baby and share in that same bonding experience.

What Jen did for me was to nurse Micah on a nursing pillow and then let me hold him. He'd inevitably fall asleep there, and when he did, Jen would transfer both the pillow and Micah over to me. Many nights I sat on the couch with that Boppy pillow around my waist and Micah fast asleep. I remember it was one of the first nights we were home. Jen nursed Micah to sleep, transferred him and the pillow to me and went upstairs to get ready for bed. While it was just the two of us, I just stared at him—watching him sleep, watching him inhale/exhale—and stroked his little head. That night I whispered to him how much I loved him, how happy I was that he was my son, how I would never leave him; I would always take care of him, protect him, teach him, play with him; and I would introduce him to the Lord. I said those things over and over. It was my way of finding my role and bonding with my son.

Encouragement for Mothers Who Breast-feed

You might be the type of mom who breast-feeds her baby *maybe* for a week. Or you might breast-feed for a month. Perhaps you plan on nursing your child until he is past two years, like I did. Any amount of time you are able to nurse will benefit both you and your baby tremendously. Did you know that you burn an extra 300 calories a day simply by breast-feeding? That adds up to 9,000 calories a month, or the equivalent of about four pounds. But more importantly, breast-feeding provides essential nutrients and antibodies to your baby, is easier for your baby to digest (especially important for a premature baby), and helps ward off disease.

The way I see it, God did a great job of designing mother's milk for her baby; so I was thrilled to be able to breast-feed Micah. It was much easier for me than waking myself up in the middle of the night to walk into the kitchen, put together a bottle, heat it to the correct temperature, feed the baby and then clean up afterward. Instead, I simply rolled over, picked up my baby from his co-sleeper that was attached to my bed right next to me and laid there while I nursed him.

Some moms love to nurse but find they are having challenges staying with it. If this is the case, don't feel bad or get discouraged. I promise you that your baby does not judge you, and neither do I. As an encouragement, I've listed 10 tips to help you be successful at breast-feeding.

Ten Tips for Successful Breast-feeding

1. Seek help from your mom, a friend or a lactation counselor who has had experience with nursing. Your hospital should provide you with a lactation counselor if you need help; or if you had your baby at home, your midwife should be more than happy to help you.

2. Use the La Leche League website for tips, online chats, forum help, and more. Consider taking a La Leche League class or joining a group (see www.llli.org).

3. Ask your husband to support your decision.

4. Sleep near your baby so that you can easily meet his or her needs.

5. Don't watch the clock; listen to your baby's needs. If he or she is hungry, it's time to be fed. There were times when Micah was teething or not feeling well that he wanted to nurse almost every hour! Was it exhausting? Yes, but it was so worth it for my child.

6. Create a comfortable place to nurse, such as a special rocking chair, a favorite place on the couch or in your bed. When I sat in my special chair or on the coach, I loved using the Boppy and the My Brest Friend nursing pillows. They helped make it so much easier to get Micah into the proper nursing position. (My favorite baby items, which I loved and couldn't live without, are listed on my website www.prayforyourbaby.com under the tab "Baby Top 10.")

7. Make sure you get your baby to latch on correctly. See www.askdrsears.com for doctor's instructions on positioning and latching.

8. To encourage your baby to nurse, do not supplement with bottles unless absolutely necessary.

9. Drink plenty of water throughout the day, and while you are nursing, to support your body's milk production.

10. Surround yourself with people who support you, and don't worry about what others think. I would nurse on the go wherever we went, but I always covered up with a little baby blanket. Now you can buy a nursing cover-up, if you prefer.

Another tip is to teach your child a cue or sound when you are going to nurse him/her. I made a soft sound similar to a clicking call for a horse. This taught my baby to turn his head and open his mouth for feeding. This way, in the middle of the night when he wanted to feed, I made that sound and then easily attached him without ever having to turn on the light.

One of my favorite books that I have sitting on my bookshelf is *The Complete Book of Christian Parenting and Child Care,* by Martha Sears, R.N., and William Sears, M.D. Dr. Sears is a Harvard-educated pediatrician with more than 30 years' experience, and Martha is a childbirth educator and breast-feeding consultant. They both highly recommend breast-feeding and present pages and pages of detailed information about feeding your baby. (Also see #7 of "Ten Tips for Successful Breast-feeding" for the website address.)

As much of a fan as I am of breast-feeding, I am fully aware that there are valid reasons why women might bottle-feed instead.

Encouragement for Mothers Who Bottle-feed

For a variety of physical and medical reasons, some women cannot breast-feed. If you are one of those women, you are just as good and loving a mother as you would be if you were feeding differently. I've heard of women who felt depressed because they were unable to breast-feed, and that is not right. Your self-esteem and your value as a mother are not dependent on *how* you feed your baby. Your baby will bond to you and love you either way.

You might need to bottle-feed because you must go back to work, or because you are raising a baby for another mom who died or one who cannot raise her own child. To you, I say, "God bless you." The important thing is that your baby receives nutrition so he or she can grow up to be a servant of God.

When bottle-feeding, it's preferable to use commercially prepared formula rather than a homemade formula, because it is manufactured under sterile conditions and contains a complex combination of proteins, sugars, fats and vitamins that would be virtually impossible to create at home.

Here are three positive points to bottle-feeding:

1. Baby formula digests slower than breast milk, so your baby will probably sleep for longer stretches at night.

2. You don't need to worry about privacy when you feed your baby in public.

3. You don't need to worry about something you eat affecting your baby's digestion, although many babies are sensitive to cow's milk, so you may have to find a formula that agrees with your baby if he or she has digestive problems or is colicky.

The time you spend feeding your baby is a natural way for mother-baby bonding, but there are many other ways you can bond with your baby.

Bonding with Your Baby

God designed mothers and infants to create a strong attachment to one another. He intended moms and new babies to be together. I remember that when Micah was a newborn, I rarely put him down. I didn't have a baby carrier at the time, so I held him in one arm while I cleaned, cooked or folded clothes with the other arm. I held him for hours on end. I *craved* holding him so much that I actually developed tendonitis in both of my wrists. By the time my second baby, Malia, was born, I got a baby carrier!

If you notice that your baby is developing a flat spot on his or her head, he or she is probably being left to lie for long periods of time. You can prevent that from happening by holding your baby more, and a baby carrier is a wonderful aid.

As many scientific studies have shown, touch is vitally important to a baby's wellbeing. For example, an interesting article in the *Developmental Psychology* newsletter states, "Overall, infants who get massage therapy gain more weight, sleep better, relate better to parents, and infant's brain waves indicate more alertness."[1] Massage therapy for babies was simply "delicately stroking" the baby's head, neck, back, legs and feet. In other words, loving touch.

This idea of touch as critical to wellbeing intrigued me, so I did more research on the topic and found that massage is also an effective tool to improve a baby's digestion, behavior and even self-esteem. "Research shows that babies receiving extra touch become better organized. They sleep better at night, fuss less during the day and relate better to caregivers' interactions. Touch settles babies."[2] In addition, "being touched gives value to a person, like an adult feeling 'touched' by the remarks of a friend."[3] So many times massage helped me put Micah back to sleep or get the gas out of his tummy, which can cause colic.[4]

You can also connect both emotionally and spiritually to your baby by singing to him or her. Your baby already knows your voice from pre-birth (as we discussed in *Praying Through Your Pregnancy*), so he or she will continue to respond to you. And who knows at what age your baby can sense the presence of the Holy Spirit? Babies feel stress, so why not God's presence? Scripture tells us this about John the Baptist: "He will also be filled with the Holy Spirit, even from his mother's womb" (Luke 1:15). I encourage you to sing your favorite hymns and gospel songs to your baby. Although I don't have a great voice, I did this with both of my babies, and now they love to sing praises to our Lord and King.

You might want to pray the following Parent's Prayer aloud so that your sweet little one can hear you. It's never too early to be a role model of trust in our heavenly Father.

Parent's Prayer

Dear Heavenly Father,

Please watch over my most precious baby as I lay her/him down each night. Surround my baby with Your angels as she/he sleeps. Let no harm come to her/him. Let her/him be blessed with dreams from You, Lord. As my baby sleeps, give me rest so that I might be a good mother/father tomorrow.

Help me make the right decision, for me, when it comes to feeding my baby. Help this baby grow healthy and strong with the milk I give her/him. Nourish this baby's body and soul like only You can, Jesus. Give me complete peace about this decision I've made, and help my friends and family to support me.

Jesus, help me bond with my baby as You intended. Give me a strong desire to hold, cuddle and love my baby each and every day. I want to be there for my baby and take care of all of her/his needs. Please give me the endurance to get through these wonderful but tiring months ahead.

Thank You, Jesus, for this gift and for Your love and grace.

In Your holy name I pray, amen.

Scriptures for Thought and Meditation

Yet you brought me out of the womb; you made me feel secure on my mother's breast.
PSALM 22:9, TNIV

As a mother comforts her child, so will I comfort you; and you will be comforted over Jerusalem.
ISAIAH 66:13, NIV

My Journal

I chose to nurse (or bottle-feed) our baby because:

_____
_____
_____
_____
_____
_____
_____
_____
_____
_____

While I fed you, I prayed about:

_____
_____
_____
_____
_____
_____
_____
_____
_____
_____
_____

Notes
1. "Infant Touch Is Critical," *Developmental Psychology,* Mesa Community College Psychology Department, Mesa, Arizona. http://www.mesacc.edu/dept/d46/psy/dev/fall00/Neonataltouch/benefits.html.
2. William Sears, M.D., and Martha Sears, *The Baby Book* (New York: Little, Brown & Co., 2003), pp. 93-94.
3. Ibid., p. 94.
4. You can find out exactly how to give your baby a massage at: http://www.makeway forbaby.com/massages.htm.

4

When Baby Cries

Jennifer's Journal

This has been a hard week. Micah is so fussy. He's just not like himself. He's drooling a lot and has a slight fever. I wonder if he's teething?

It doesn't feel right letting him cry it out like some people have told me to do. I'm not that kind of mom, and it truly goes against my motherly instincts. He's almost three months old, and I know that I'm supposed to be his comforter.

Well, I'm not going to let him cry it out. I'm going to pick him up and hold him, no matter what. I know if I were that little and something was wrong, I would want my mom to hold me.

Lord, please help me understand my baby's cries and what they mean. I want him to be happy and feel loved, all the time.

Micah was a very happy baby and rarely cried. Now jump ahead two-and-a-half years to March 2008, and Micah is now a toddler, and my daughter, Malia, has just been born. I've been by myself for over a week now because my husband is working three jobs so that I can be a stay-at-home mom. Malia is just 10 days old, and I feel like I'm losing it. She cries incessantly every time I change her, and she needs her diaper changed six to eight times *an hour!* Every time I change her, she screams. Then I start crying, and I try to wipe her quickly and cover her back up so I can nurse her. This time, right before I put her new diaper back on, I notice that she has *no skin* left on her bottom.

I was so exhausted after being up most of the night changing her every hour that I didn't even notice her raw bottom. I felt absolutely terrible. *What kind of mother am I?* I immediately took her to the doctor, who assured me that I'm a great mom and that Malia must be allergic to the baby wipes I'm using; in addition, she must have a tummy bug. Instead of using wipes for the next week, the doctor wanted me to use a squirt bottle like they give you in the hospital. I'm to put clean warm water in it mixed with one tablespoon of baking soda. Then I need to rinse her off each time, and then let her air dry for a few minutes before I dress her.

I gladly accepted the doctor's advice and ran home to set up my new changing station on the floor of the living room. I gathered a blanket, a bunch of soft dish-size towels, the squirt bottle, baking soda, natural diaper cream and the blow dryer. Every 10 to 20 minutes, I went through the process of cleaning off the diarrhea, blow-drying her on low (because it was winter and I didn't want her to get cold), applying the diaper cream and then getting her dressed all over again. Through it all, I kept thinking, *How could I have let this happen to her?*

I share this story to let you know that sometimes a mom doesn't understand what her baby is trying to tell her. I was so exhausted as I changed Malia over and over in dim light during the night that I didn't realize what had happened to her little bottom. My encouragement here is to help you learn to understand your baby's cries so you can have a much happier home.

Crying is the only language a newborn knows. If babies didn't cry, some of them would not survive; so it's a good thing that crying is not a skill that has to be learned. In the beginning, babies have *many* needs, and they have only one way of asking to have those needs met. When a baby cries, it is the parent's responsibility to try to figure out the need.

How to Help a Crying Baby

A baby has different cries for different needs, and once you learn how to be sensitive to those various sounds, it's a lot easier to make your baby happy. Here are eight common questions to ask yourself to help determine what your baby needs.

1. Is My Baby Hungry?

This is the most obvious reason a baby cries. A newborn needs to eat *often,* so I recommend throwing out a schedule, especially if you are nursing. Your baby will probably need to be fed more often than if you are bottle-feeding, because mother's milk is more quickly digested. But if you know your baby cannot be hungry, then look at the rest of the list for possible reasons he or she might be uncomfortable.

2. Is My Baby Tired?

If your baby's cry sounds something like a yawn at first, with his or her mouth opened in an O shape, he or she might need to sleep. I usually nursed my little ones to sleep at this age, but you can also try carrying your baby around in a front pack carrier or just holding and rocking him or her to sleep.

3. Does My Baby Need to Be Burped?

If you recently fed your baby and he didn't get to burp, you can try again. Sometimes a repetitive staccato cry is a code for, "I need to be burped, please." Many people encouraged me to pat my kids pretty hard to get the burps out, but there's a better way. My friend Betty, who is a massage therapist and a mother of three, suggested that I make clockwise circles on Micah's back, pressing gently on the way up. This worked every time and was more appropriate for a newborn.

4. Does My Baby Need a Diaper Change?

A wet or dirty diaper can cause diaper rash, so you'll want to keep your baby's bottom dry and comfortable. I learned this firsthand with Micah, and I wish I had remembered it with Malia. But her condition that included the stomach virus was rare, and her rash was quickly remedied with the baking soda-water mix and natural Burt's Bees Diaper Ointment.

5. Is My Baby in Pain?

Babies get gas in their intestines, and this hurts. If burping doesn't help, try placing her facedown and gently rubbing her back. If that doesn't help, try motion, such as a baby swing, rocking, or walking with your baby in your arms. Sometimes infants can get tummy cramps or infant constipation as well. Here are some ideas you can try:

- *Tummy massage:* Gently massage and rub baby's tummy in a clockwise direction. Place your hands at baby's navel and massage in a circular motion, moving your hands out and away from the center of baby's belly. I did this with both of my babies and it helped them so much.

- *Bicycle legs:* Place your baby on her back and lightly hold her legs in a half-bent position. Gently begin to move your baby's legs as if she is riding a bicycle. Alternate "bicycle legs" with tummy massage. Bicycle legs also may help to relieve a baby who is gassy.

- *A warm bath:* Some medical professionals suggest giving your constipated baby a warm bath. The idea is to help relax the baby and "get things moving" again. Give a tummy massage in the tub or while you are drying baby.[1]

6. Is My Baby Too Hot or Too Cold?

This is a quick and easy fix. Always try to dress your baby in light layers. This way you can easily peel off one layer at a time if you feel your baby perspire. Micah liked to get bundled up with lots of blankets, but Malia disliked having any covers on her. To this day, each night when I check on her in her little bed, she's lying in the fetal position with no covers, freezing cold, but she loves it. I often cover her and come back to check on her 20 minutes later, only to find she has kicked off the covers again.

7. Is My Baby in an Uncomfortable Position?

One mother said she couldn't figure out why her baby was crying. He'd just been changed, fed and burped, and everything seemed to be good. Then she changed his position, and he immediately stopped crying. She remembers saying to him, "If I'd only known that was what you wanted, I would have turned you sooner."

Malia always let me know that she absolutely hated being in the car seat. Every time we went somewhere, she screamed. It made driving with her for the first year very stressful indeed. The doctor said the position she was in must hurt her tummy and cause acid reflux. This was one of those things I really couldn't do anything about; safety came first. I can't tell you how happy I was when she was old enough for me to turn her car seat around, and she stopped screaming. Praise God!

8. Does My Baby Need Some TLC?

Babies need lots of tender loving care. You might be able to make your baby happy simply by holding her and letting her hear your voice. A baby recognizes his or her mother's voice even before birth. Don't worry about "spoiling" your baby by holding her too much, because that's not possible at the infant stage. Being touched and cuddled is a genuine need, and meeting this need helps a baby develop the ability to bond and form relationships with other people later in life. Pediatricians say that you can never spoil an infant; your baby cannot "control" you; and studies have shown that excessive crying can be harmful to the baby's cardio-vascular and respiratory system.[2]

It can be puzzling to figure out why your baby is crying, but hang in there and soon you'll be able to tell when your little one is hungry, wet, in pain or just needs to be held.

Nana's Journal

I remember how exhausting being a new mother can be, so I try to help my daughter or daughter-in-law when there's a new baby in the family.

I remember my own mother coming to visit after my babies were born. I felt so grateful when she cleaned the kitchen and folded the laundry. So I try to pass on that help to my own kids.

Of course, I love to hold my new grandchild, and I believe doing so creates good grandchild-grandparent bonding. It also gives the new mommy a chance to take a shower or nap without worrying about the baby needing something, as she knows I'm there to give tender loving care.

In addition, our church has a ministry to new mothers. Volunteers prepare and deliver dinner to the family for a few days after the birth. This is a ministry of helps, as it's called in 1 Corinthians 12:28, and it is a wonderful blessing to the family.

Carolyn Warren

Clearing Up the Mystery of Colic

Colic is a convenient word for "unexplained crying." Fortunately, neither Micah nor Malia had colic; but in researching this topic, I found two physical causes and one emotional cause. Here's what current medical science has to say.

First, *your baby might be sensitive or intolerant to a substance in your milk or in a particular baby formula.* Some common allergens you may want to avoid are dairy, gas-producing vegetables, citrus fruits and juice, caffeine, eggs, decongestants and certain medicines.

To pinpoint exactly what your baby may be allergic to, do an elimination diet one item at a time. When I ate shrimp, Micah would be up all night, tossing and turning. I found this out by eliminating shrimp from my diet for a long while and then trying it again—and boy we both paid for it! We were both up all night, Micah crying and me dancing with him to try to calm him down.

If you're bottle-feeding, try switching to a formula made specifically for babies with sensitive digestive systems. Most brands offer a formula for colicky babies (check their websites).

Second, *your baby may have gastroesophageal reflux, or GER*. Babies can get GER when they have a poorly coordinated gastrointestinal tract. They will manifest painful crying and will spit up. You can get your baby tested with a simple pH level test for the esophagus.

Third, *your baby may have a very sensitive disposition or temperament and be experiencing disorganized biorhythms*. If this is the case, try to create a calm, stress-free atmosphere. Try to hold your baby as much as possible. Play slow, soothing music and dance with your baby in different directions. You can also hold your baby in a sling so you can carry him or her around with you throughout the day as much as possible. In addition, keep loud harsh sounds— such as yelling, arguing and violent television—out of your home.

While I was writing this chapter on comforting a crying baby, I thought of Psalm 57:2-3: "I cry out to God Most High, to God who performs all things for me. He shall send from heaven and save me. . . . God shall send forth His mercy and His truth." To me that is a perfect example of how our heavenly Father responds to our cries. What does He do? He sends love and faithfulness, and that is how we can respond to our baby's cries as well. With loving care, we faithfully take care of our baby's needs.

Parent's Prayer

Dear Lord God,
Thank You for my precious new baby. Thank You for this love
I have for him/her. Thank You for showing me the depth of Your

own love through being a parent. I am coming to understand Your unconditional love as I never have before. Continue to reveal Your love to me.

Help me understand what my baby needs when he/she cries. Give me good parental instincts to know what to do. I don't want to ever overlook any genuine need. Make me calm so I can pass on peace to my child.

God, I have to be honest: sometimes I am just too tired. Please give me a deep and peaceful sleep at night so that I can wake up feeling refreshed. Help my baby sleep at night when I need to sleep, but also help me feel at peace when it's time to wake up for his/her nightly feedings.

In Jesus' name, amen.

Scriptures for Thought and Meditation

Come to Me, all you who labor and are heavy laden, and I will give you rest.
MATTHEW 11:28

Be anxious for nothing, but in everything by prayer and supplication, let your requests be made known to God; and the peace of God, which surpasses all understanding, will guard your hearts and minds through Christ Jesus.
PHILIPPIANS 4:6-7

My Journal

As a baby, when you cried out to me, here's what I did to help calm you:

_____

_____

_____

_____

_____
_____
_____
_____
_____
_____
_____
_____
_____
_____
_____
_____
_____

What I have learned about love from my baby so far:

_____
_____
_____
_____
_____
_____
_____
_____
_____
_____
_____
_____
_____
_____
_____
_____
_____
_____

Notes

1. "Constipation and Your Baby," April 2, 2011. http://wholesomebabyfood.momtastic.com/constip.htm (accessed June 2012).
2. William Sears and Martha Sears, *The Complete Book of Christian Parenting & Child Care* (Nashville, TN: Broadman & Holman Publishers, 1997), p. 211.

5

Preventing Mommy Burnout:
Taking Care of Your Soul, Body and Spirit

Jennifer's Journal

Micah is three and a half months old. It's 5:30 in the afternoon, and I still haven't taken a shower. All he wants to do is nurse today. I wonder if he doesn't feel very well or if he's teething, because he sure is drooling a lot. The house is a mess, and I'm exhausted. We were up most of the night as well. I haven't worked out as much lately, but at least I'm still walking a lot and carrying a 12-pound baby around with me all day long. Micah has almost doubled his weight already. Our doctor is very happy and says she can't believe he was ever in the NICU.

I do miss going to the gym and working out each day, so I brought Micah with me to the Rec Center to try to do 30 minutes of weights. He sits so nicely in the stroller, so I thought it was a perfect idea. Well, it was, until one of the trainers said kids aren't allowed up there. Oh well, I can do it at home.

I can't believe next month is Christmas. Yesterday, we put up our big tree. Maybe that's why I'm so tired. It's takes us three days to decorate just the inside of the house. But Dan loves Christmas so much, and it's important to us that Micah learns the true meaning about why we celebrate Jesus' birth . . . but I think I'd better slow down and have some "me time" soon.

Avoiding mommy burnout is tough to do if you're like I was: all alone with a new baby and very little help. With my parents in Hawaii and my siblings scattered around the world, and Dan's family living out of state, we had no family near us, and we couldn't afford to hire a nanny or mother's helper. Dan was gone all the time, working three jobs, so it was just Micah and me keeping up with cooking, cleaning, laundry and diaper changing. It's amazing when I think about how much free time I had before he was born; I never realized how much time I wasted on TV, shopping or excessive working out.

As new moms, we need total support: soul, body and spirit. So I'm addressing all three of these areas next.

Taking Care of Your Soul: Join a Support Group

I recommend joining a group of Christian moms who, like you, have a baby or young child and need support. MOPS (Mothers of Pre-schoolers) is an international Christian organization set up in most parts of the United States and around the world. In spite of the name, they allow all new moms who have children from birth to six years old to join their organization.

I wish I'd known about MOPS when Micah was born. I joined when he was four years old and Malia was one-and-a-half. The women in my group were fun and understanding and supportive of one another. Our particular MOPS group meets twice a month at our church. They offer childcare, brunch, interesting speakers and, above all, a way to connect with other moms who are going through the same daily drama. I can't say enough positive things about MOPS for new moms, so I'll let some MOPS leaders speak for themselves.

Daddy's Blog

I have to tell you, I didn't do such a great job at helping Jen avoid burnout. Not only did I not understand it, but she also didn't find it easy to communicate what she needed.

Like most men, I wanted to tell her, "Just power through it!" which is what she usually does, but this was different. After all, that's what we do as guys, but I am constantly reminded that a woman doesn't work that way. If I could do it over again, here are some things I would have done differently:

- Changed more diapers.
- Taken the baby off her hands for 30 minutes so she could take a shower or bath each day.
- Offered to bring in a housekeeper to help with all the work. (If this is not in your budget, maybe you could find some time to do the chores yourself.)
- Told her she's beautiful and that I love her. (I know what you're thinking, *I told her that when we got married; if anything changes I will let her know.* Unfortunately, that old joke doesn't work very well for a successful marriage.)
- Sent her a note or text message to say she's a great mom and she's doing a great job.

Finally, some women just need to talk, and that alone helps them avoid burnout. My error was that I would listen and then try to fix it. As hard as it is to comprehend, women do not always want us to fix them. They just want us to listen. I will never know why that is until I get to heaven, but just trust me that it's a fact.

Alexandra Kuykendall,
Mom and Lead Content Editor for MOPS

Alexandra Kuykendall, who calls herself a diaper changer, dinner maker, tear wiper, laundry hater, family lover and MOPS promoter said, "First and foremost, I want all moms who come to a MOPS group to know that what they are going through is normal, not unique.

"When a mom joins MOPS, she meets other women right next to her who are going through the same things she is, and those women can offer coping ideas she may not have thought of.

"Each group also has what we call Mentor Moms. These are women who are done with the early years of raising their children. They help the moms with young children by sharing fresh ideas to help us live through the hard days and by reassuring us that life will get easier. It's not always going to be like it is now, with diapers and laundry on the floor of every room in your house."

I had to laugh, because it's so true. I asked Alexandra to share her personal MOPS experience, and here is her story:

When I moved to Denver 10 years ago, I didn't know a single person. I was five months pregnant, and I felt isolated and very much alone. Finally, when my baby was nine months old, I joined the MOPS group at my church. It saved me! That group provided me with friendships and a purpose outside of diaper duty. I quickly got into a leadership position, and doing so enabled me to use parts of myself that weren't being used in mothering.

It made me feel like I was contributing to God's kingdom by using my other talents. Also, one of the best things about MOPS was that it gave me encouragement, practical support and real friends—friends I could call on at any time when I was having a hard moment.

MOPS also supports women in their spiritual journey. If a mom comes to MOPS having never prayed before, she will find role models from her peers. *Our hope is that we bring every mother one step closer to Jesus, no matter where she is in her faith journey. It is our goal that when she enters MOPS, she will be strengthened in her faith.* And if she's never heard about Jesus, our prayer is that she will become interested in who He is. On the other hand, if she has a strong faith, then she will be offered leadership opportunities.

MOPS is for *every* mom. Our group experience and the core of our ministry is to serve other women. You truly learn to love your neighbor as yourself and put it into practice. Even if you're exhausted, you can be challenged to reach out to someone who is even more exhausted than yourself.

Interview with Elisa Morgan
President Emerita, MOPS International;
Publisher, Fulfill; and 2012 Women of Faith Speaker

JP: *Will you tell our readers how you see moms today?*

Elisa: I like to use the metaphor of a juice box. Instead of using just one straw, moms nowadays have 15 straws. Everyone comes and takes a drink from her all day long. Moms are constantly filling up everyone else. But mothers can't continue to fill others up when they themselves are sucked dry. It's not selfish to pay attention to self-care—it's a necessity. You can't give to others what you don't have yourself. So, moms, you need to remember to take care of yourself first.

JP: *Right now, it seems that so many new moms are completely overwhelmed with raising their children, taking care of their homes—and some are working full-time or part-time, as well. What can these women who are experiencing what I call "Mommy burnout" do to help themselves?*

Elisa: I would say to prayerfully discern what they are supposed to be doing during this season of life. Are they supposed to do it all, or take time out from something else in their life? Discernment is letting some things go and picking other things up. They need to ask, "How much time and energy am I supposed to spend, and where should I spend it?"

JP: *That's wonderful advice! And what can a mom do to take care of her soul?*

Elisa: The season of mothering young children is still a season that oftentimes moms forget they are still developing in their own selves. There are several times in life when moms are especially open to their own spiritual needs, and motherhood is one of those times, because they are so aware of their responsibility. This is a developmental season for a mom to define and discover her faith. I encourage mothers to dig into it, because their children are going to look to them to be the Hope Bringer. So, a mom can ask herself, What do I have to share with them? God does not want us to mother alone. We need to ask the questions, Do I allow God to lead me through my parenting? Through being a mom, do I share Jesus with my family? There is a huge misconception that we moms are supposed to do this alone; but we need God to walk alongside us at this time.

JP: *Yes, that is so important, to ask God to walk alongside us as moms. Is there anything else you want to leave with our readers on how to take care of themselves during this trying, yet wonderful, time in their lives?*

Elisa: I would tell them that being a mom doesn't mean you stop being a woman! Pay attention to your ongoing discovery of who you are. What are your strengths, your weaknesses and your talents? What experiences do you have, and what do you want to do in the future? What do you not want to do? Give yourself permission to dream and to keep building the rest of yourself. Moms are moms—but they are also much more . . . and we often forget that.

To locate a MOPS group near you, go to www.mops.org and click on Find a Group. If there is not a MOPS group near you, click on Start a New Group to access all the resources you need to do that. You can also contact your church and ask if they have any other mommy groups or ladies Bible studies you could join. If you're in a small church without a support group, then check out a nearby larger church. They'll welcome you into their midweek group even if you attend Sunday services elsewhere.

Please stay connected. My biggest mistake was thinking that I could do it all on my own. In the beginning, I didn't think I'd fit into a group of ladies like that, but my friend persuaded me to try it, and I'm sure glad I did.

The wisdom of Scripture tells us, "Two are better than one, because they have a good reward for their labor: For if they fall, one will lift up his companion. But woe to him who is alone when he falls, for he has no one to help him up" (Eccles. 4:9-10). When you're in a support group, you have friends who can catch you when you're about to fall. As moms together, we can relate to one another's feelings and be sensitive to one another.

The apostle Paul instructs us to "Bear one another's burdens, and so fulfill the law of Christ" (Gal. 6:2). God clearly does not want us to go through this special time in our lives alone. God is specific about saying that we are social beings who need others. I love to read Romans 12:15, where the Holy Spirit says, "Rejoice with those who rejoice, and weep with those who weep." We need friends to share in the good times and the bad, both to laugh with and cry with.

Taking Care of Your Body: Proper Nutrition

In the prologue of this book, I mentioned that I've been a nutrition and fitness coach for more than 20 years. I love to teach moms about the importance of food and how it affects their bodies, and their babies' bodies as well, if they are nursing. I'm not going to go overboard in this book about nutrition and exercise. My husband and I created *The Great Shape-Up Program*—complete instructions with a book, CD and DVD (a complete package so that you can do the exercises right along with us) for proper nutrition and exercises to get your pre-baby body back, or even better. But I would like to share the best practices that worked for me. Feel free to steal my ideas for yourself.

Eating healthy doesn't have to be a burden to be a way of life. When God created the earth and mankind, people weren't eating processed foods loaded with high-fructose corn syrup, chemicals, preservatives, dyes and other unhealthy ingredients. It was a simpler time, a time when God provided the plants and seeds and the healthy meat, fish and fowl to eat. When we go back to basics and eat the healthy, whole foods that provide protein and nutrients, we feel better. I know this firsthand, because I didn't always eat healthy during my college years.

After graduating, I decided to change the way I ate, and I started working out. Consequently, I lost 40 pounds right away. I've kept if off for more than 20 years now, and I try to always choose what's good for my body. This gives me more energy and keeps me at a healthy weight. For a new mom, eating right is part of the formula for feeling good and avoiding excessive fatigue and eventual burnout.

One possible stumbling block to healthy eating is being overly busy and overly tired. When you're waking up at night to feed your baby, it's only natural to feel tired during the day. The lurking temptation is to pick up fast food or a candy bar, even though you know they are high in fat and empty calories. So how do you avoid those pitfalls and prevent the formation of bad habits and unhealthy food cravings?

Here are my best secrets for keeping healthy and energetic, even as a busy parent. It doesn't take a lot of time each day—just try to be as consistent as you can and try to prepare ahead if possible. The next thing you know, you will be living a healthy lifestyle.

Jennifer's Ten Best Tips to Be a Healthy, Energetic New Mom

1. Exercise Three to Five Days in the Week
For me, this included doing simple things such as taking Micah for a 20-minute walk. I packed him in the Baby Bjorn or the jogging stroller when the weather permitted us to get outdoors. (Getting outside is refreshing in itself.) Or, I sat on the living room floor and did yoga stretches and abdominal work, like sit-ups. On alternate days, I worked with simple free weights while Micah slept nearby in his baby Moses basket.

2. Make Special Smoothies
Making my special smoothies twice a day was one of the easiest things I did to help me drop the pregnancy pounds and feel great.

It only takes about five minutes to have a complete meal that is both nutritious and delicious.

Jennifer's Healthy Smoothie

1 to 2 cups milk (rice, almond or skim milk—try to avoid soy right now because of your hormones)

1 to 2 scoops rice, egg or whey protein powder (available at any natural grocery store)

1 frozen banana

1 to 2 cups frozen fruit (try mangos, peaches, strawberries, pineapple, blueberries or any other fruit you love—I recommend organic fruit to avoid chemicals)

Blend all ingredients together and pour into a tall glass. Leftover smoothie can be frozen into popsicles.

3. Do a Combo Cardio Walk

This is the best exercise routine for a mom to do while carrying her baby in a front baby carrier. Your baby's weight does the work of free weights. This is an effective workout that doesn't require a gym membership or the purchase of any special equipment. You'll be pleased at how this routine takes off unwanted pounds and makes you feel fantastic.

Jennifer's Outdoor Combo Workout Routine

Step #1: Five minutes of brisk walking while carrying baby in a front baby carrier.

Step #2: Do 10 to 20 walking lunges on an even surface, such as a path. Just watch your form and always keep your toes in line with your knees when you lunge.

Step #3: Pick up the pace by walking another five minutes.

Step #4: Stop walking and do 10 to 20 squats. You can hold on to a tree for balance.

Repeat all steps 2 to 3 times.

After this workout, when I got home, I did three sets of 15 push-ups (on your knees is fine until you work up to a full push-up) and five minutes of abdominal work and stretching. If you weren't used to exercising before your baby was born, then you might need to work up to this full routine. On a scale of 1 to 10, your perceived exertion level should be between 4 and 6. As always, follow your doctor's orders, especially if you had a C-section or any medical complications.

4. Exercise Inside the Home

During harsh winter weather or hot weather, I did a lot of exercising inside my home. Micah was too young to take out of the house into the cold, freezing air, so I popped in a yoga tape or walked around the house doing lunges, then I stopped to do squats and push-ups, and then I did abs for about five minutes. Sometimes I would listen to Christian radio or Christian music on my iPod, or I'd blast it through the house and sing to Micah as I exercised. Adding music to exercise makes the time fly.

5. Drink, Drink, and Drink More Water!

I know that you may have heard this a thousand times before, but it cannot be overstated. Water not only hydrates your body, but it also flushes out toxins. Drinking water is also a must if you are nursing. You will want to avoid sodas and other sugary beverages, because they are unhealthy, provide no vitamins or essential nutrients and add empty calories.[1] Often when people are dehydrated, they think that they need sugar or caffeine, but their bodies are actually crying out for water. So go grab a glass right now!

6. Drink Herbal Tea

For a morning wake-up, sometimes I have a cup or two of herbal tea with one to two teaspoons of my favorite honey. I'm not a morning person at all, but I do not drink coffee or any type of caffeine to wake myself up. Instead, I enjoy herbal tea such as Celestial Seasonings peppermint, blueberry, black cherry, peach or any of their fruity flavors and stir in a teaspoon of Lehua honey. I think it's the best honey in the world. It comes from bees in Hawaii that gather nectar almost exclusively from the Ohia Lehua blossom. During the winter months, I drink it hot; and during summer, I drink it iced. (If you don't live in Hawaii, you can find Lehua honey at www.bigislandbees.com or other websites online.)

7. Eat a Quick and Healthy Midday Snack
For a midday snack, I enjoy a handful of dry roasted almonds, cashews or walnuts. Or I have plain yogurt with sugar-free granola, such as Udi's.

8. Be Prepared for Hunger
When I'm away from home and get hungry, I have LäraBars, raw or dry roasted nuts, dried fruit and water in my car so I never go hungry. If you're not familiar with LäraBars, they are made with 100 percent natural food with no chemicals, fillers, processing or added sugar. They are free of gluten, dairy, soy, GMO foods, cholesterol and sodium. You certainly can't say that about the junk they try to pass off as food in the snack aisle or in drive-thru chains.

9. Avoid Temptation at Home
I find that the best way to avoid eating the wrong things is to keep healthy food ready to eat (strawberries washed and cut or veggies washed and cut into sticks and stored in little bags). I place these at eye level in my fridge so they are the first things I see. Also, I don't buy junk food, so it's not in my house. If my husband needs an ice cream "fix," I ask him to do it outside the house. And now that we have children, if he wants a treat, he has it *after* they go to bed. Our secret code is "I'm going to the bank," which really means he is going to Dairy Queen.

10. Eat a Quick and Healthy Dinner
A good example of a quick dinner after a busy day is a yummy yet healthy pizza. Everyone in my family enjoys this, especially the kids.

Jennifer's Easy Healthy Pizza

One 12-inch whole wheat or spelt tortilla topped with the following:

2 tablespoons pesto (we love the Costco brand)
½ cup shredded zucchini, olives, sundried tomatoes, mushrooms or veggies of your choice
½ cup spinach leaves, chopped
1 cup leftover cooked chicken
1 cup cheese (rice, almond or low-fat cheese)

Spread all ingredients on tortilla in the order listed. Bake directly on the wire rack at 350° F for 8 to 10 minutes. (Note: When my children were infants, sometimes I laid out six tortillas and made a lot of pizzas at once. I froze the extras in tinfoil and a large gallon-size Ziploc bag. That way, I had two extra meals ready for another day when the baby had a "needy day," or I was just too tired to cook.)

In addition, here is the grocery list I created for myself and my clients. Check off what you need before going grocery shopping. It works wonders for staying on the right track while you're in the store. When you make the right food choices while shopping, you'll set yourself up for success in eating foods that provide your body with energy, nutrition and good health at home.

Grocery List

Note: The servings listed are per day. Foods that are 100 percent organic, free-range, non-antibiotic, hormone-free and non-GMO foods are best! The servings are listed.

Dairy
1–2 servings; low-fat or nonfat/protein

❑ Egg whites
❑ Milk (Skim, rice, coconut or almond milk is preferred)
❑ Light margarine
❑ Sour cream
❑ Tofu (firm is better)

- [ ] Yogurt (plain is best)
- [ ] Cottage cheese
- [ ] Ricotta cheese
- [ ] Hard cheese
- [ ] Goat milk or goat cheese

Meat, Fish, Poultry and Proteins
4–6 servings/protein

- [ ] Chicken breasts
- [ ] Turkey breasts
- [ ] Lean ground beef or buffalo
- [ ] Sliced beef pot roast
- [ ] Sirloin steak
- [ ] Shellfish (lobster, scallops, shrimp)
- [ ] Crab (Alaskan, blue)
- [ ] Fresh fish (salmon, red snapper, orange roughy, halibut, tuna, cod, haddock, grouper, swordfish, trout, snapper, mackerel)
- [ ] Elk or ostrich
- [ ] Whey, soy, rice or egg protein powder

Fruit
2–3 servings/carbohydrates

- [ ] Apples
- [ ] Bananas
- [ ] Berries
- [ ] Grapefruit
- [ ] Grapes
- [ ] Lemons and limes
- [ ] Melon
- [ ] Oranges and tangerines
- [ ] Pears
- [ ] Papaya
- [ ] Mangos
- [ ] Apricots
- [ ] Nectarines
- [ ] Kiwis
- [ ] Plums
- [ ] Cantaloupe

Vegetables
7–9 servings/carbohydrates

- [ ] Broccoli
- [ ] Cabbage
- [ ] Carrots
- [ ] Cauliflower
- [ ] Celery
- [ ] Cucumbers
- [ ] Garlic and onions
- [ ] Lettuce (no iceberg)
- [ ] Mushrooms
- [ ] Peppers
- [ ] Potatoes
- [ ] Radishes

- Tomatoes
- Asparagus
- Artichokes
- Bell peppers
- Brussels sprouts
- Eggplant
- Peas
- Collard greens and spinach
- Sweet or white potatoes
- Zucchini and yellow squash
- Beets

Breads
1–2 servings/carbohydrates

- Tortillas (whole wheat, corn or spelt)
- 12-grain bread
- Whole-wheat bread
- Whole-wheat pita bread
- Spelt, oat or rice bread

Dry Goods
1 serving/carbohydrates or fat

- Cereal (minimum 3 grams of fiber and low sugar)
- Oatmeal (whole oats)
- Whole-wheat, soy or rice pasta
- Beans, lentils or peas
- Quinoa
- Wheat germ
- Whole-wheat flour
- Whole-wheat crackers
- Baked blue corn chips
- Rice crackers
- Whole-wheat couscous
- Brown rice (basmati, jasmine or wild)
- Walnuts
- Dried fruit (such as raisins, mango or pineapple with no added sugar)
- Peanut butter (natural)
- Almonds (raw, dry roasted or almond butter)
- Ground flaxseeds or flaxseed oil
- Canola oil
- Olive oil
- Cooking spray (olive or canola)

Canned Goods (only if fresh is not available)

- Unsweetened applesauce
- Soups
- Marinara sauce
- Tomato sauce

- ☐ Tuna
- ☐ Peas, spinach, green beans, lima beans
- ☐ Garbanzo beans
- ☐ Salmon

- ☐ Black, pinto and lentil beans
- ☐ Chicken or vegetable broth (low-sodium)

Beverages
- ☐ Herbal tea (decaf; 3 to 4 cups per day)
- ☐ Bottled water (1 gallon per day)

- ☐ 100% fresh fruit or vegetable juice (8 ounces per day)

Condiments and Spices
- ☐ Mustard (Dijon)
- ☐ Salad dressings
- ☐ Salsa
- ☐ Vinegars

- ☐ Various spices
- ☐ Hummus
- ☐ Mayonnaise (canola or soy)

Frozen Foods (back-up foods)
- ☐ Fruit
- ☐ Broccoli and spinach
- ☐ Soybeans
- ☐ Vegetables

- ☐ Shrimp, fish or chicken
- ☐ Healthy frozen dinners

Taking Care of Your Spirit: Getting Refreshed

Whenever I held Micah in my arms or even stood over his bed and watched him sleep, I felt amazement for this new life God had entrusted to me. As parents, we would do anything for our children. And yet, we must take time to care for ourselves as well. Think of it this way: It will do your baby no good if you have a breakdown. Even Jesus took time out from ministering to the people who so desperately needed Him when He got up before dawn to escape the crowds and go to a private place to pray (see Mark 1:35).

Here's an encouraging promise from Isaiah 40:31:

Those who wait on the Lord shall renew their strength;
they shall mount up with wings like eagles, they shall run
and not be weary, they shall walk and not faint.

Exactly how do you wait on the Lord to receive this eagle-like
energy? One way is to play worship music while you lie down to
rest. Listen to the music, let the praises wash over your spirit, and
say, "Yes, Lord, I praise and worship You. Come, Holy Spirit." Even
15 minutes can make a difference in how you feel.

Another way is to meditate on Scripture. Think about a particular Bible verse, pray it aloud and remind yourself of it throughout the day. You might even write it down and post it on your
bathroom mirror. We've included Scriptures for this purpose at
the end of each chapter.

A third way to receive from God is to ask for prayer support.
Are there grandmas or grandpas in your church? These people
have been through a lot of life experience. Asking one of these
godly retired folks for prayer support can make a huge difference
to you and your family.

Everyone is unique, so whatever brings the Holy Spirit close
to you is a beautiful thing. And remember, taking time out to be
with God to refresh your spirit will ultimately result in a benefit
for your baby as well.

Parent's Prayer

Dear Heavenly Father,

*Today, this prayer is for me. Lord, I want to be a good mother/
father to my baby. Sometimes I feel so overwhelmed, and I need Your
help. Please surround me with friends who can support me and
lead me when I need it most. Help me to be a friend to others too.*

*Give me the desire to eat healthy foods and avoid the junk.
Give me the strength to exercise each day. I know that You want me*

to live a healthy lifestyle and teach my baby how to live one as well. It says in Your Word that my body is Your temple (see 1 Cor. 6:19); help me to make it a place where You would like to live.

And, Jesus, I pray that You will renew my spirit as I spend time with You each and every day. I want to grow our friendship and learn how to truly know You. You are my Strength and my Comforter. Thank You, Lord, for being my Friend.

In Your mighty name I pray, amen.

Scriptures for Thought and Meditation

The heartfelt counsel of a friend is as sweet as perfume and incense.
PROVERBS 27:9, NLT

Come to Me, all who labor and are heavy laden, and I will give you rest.
MATTHEW 11:28

My nutrition program includes (e.g., lots of fruits, veggies, chicken):

_____

_____

_____

_____

_____

_____

_____

_____

_____

_____

_____

_____

_____

_____

My exercise plan includes:

_____
_____
_____
_____
_____
_____
_____
_____
_____
_____
_____
_____
_____
_____
_____
_____
_____
_____
_____
_____
_____
_____
_____
_____
_____
_____
_____
_____
_____
_____
_____

Note

1. Timothy S. Harlan, "Don't Drink Soda," July 16, 2009. http://www.livestrong.com/article/14062-don-t-drink-soda/ (accessed July 2012).

6

All the Firsts for Baby!

Jennifer's Journal

I'm so excited. Micah's first tooth just broke through. He's now four-and-a-half months old, and I knew something had been going on with him the last few weeks. It's so cute to see him put his whole fist in his mouth. He makes me laugh so much. I can barely stand it. He's also starting to scoot around the house. And I know soon he'll be running down the street chasing his soccer ball. It seems like yesterday that he gave me his first real smile while we were in Hawaii, visiting my parents. He was just three-and-a-half weeks old, and I took about 10 pictures, because I didn't want Dan to miss it; he was still in Denver.

I can't believe how quickly time flies by. Lord, help me not to miss any of my baby's "firsts." I know You gave these to me as a blessing, and I want to thank You for the joy they bring me. I want to stop time right now and not have him grow up anymore.

Wouldn't it be nice to be able to freeze time and keep our children at a certain age? I absolutely loved Micah's first year. I can honestly say that year was the best year of my life. As I write this, Micah is almost seven years old, and there are times when I long to go back to that first year. Please don't take that wrong. I am very happy and blessed now that we have Malia as well, but that brand-new first year of being a mom was a very special blessing from God, and I will cherish it always.

One of the funniest baby "firsts" took place at the hospital. We were waiting for Micah's first poop. Can you imagine? We were not allowed to leave the hospital until that event, so it was a big deal. I also have fond memories of the first time he nursed. I was amazed and in awe of this little guy and so delighted that I could provide what he needed nutritionally.

I invite you to celebrate your baby's firsts, the special moments when he or she does something for the first time. At the end of this chapter, there is a place to record those events. When your child is older, it will be special to read your journal together.

Baby's First Smile

Micah smiled his first real smile when I was in Hawaii visiting my parents. During my pregnancy I had prayed for a happy child who would be full of the joy of the Lord. To see him smile at everyone, well, that was one of the first signs that let me know God had heard my prayers. It was a moment like we read about in Psalm 126:3: "The LORD has done great things for us, and we are glad."

No matter how young or old your baby is right now, you can speak blessing over him or her. You can claim joy and other blessings for your little one. You can bring a spirit of gladness and contentment into your home by praising God and reciting psalms when you change diapers and do laundry and all the other necessary daily tasks. If you ask God to be present in your son's or daughter's life and fill your little one with the joy of the Holy Spirit, I believe He will do it.

Baby's First Tooth

Both Micah and Malia got their first tooth at four-and-a-half months. But did you know that some babies are born with teeth? Isn't it interesting that God made all of our babies so unique? God cares about every little part of our babies—even their teeth. I encourage you to begin praying early on for your baby's teeth; it might save him or her a lot of complications later on.

A common question that first-time parents ask is, "At what age should I take my child for the first dental visit?" In general, most dentists recommend age two to three. However, that may vary depending on whether or not there is fluoride in your water. If not, your dentist might offer to brush your child's teeth with fluoride in the first year. I did not do this; instead, I made sure to keep their little mouths squeaky clean. Additionally, some pediatricians do a visual check on a young child's teeth, so you can wait until a little later, unless the doctor notices an issue that needs special attention.

Baby's First Rollover

I was so amazed the first time my little ones decided to roll over. We were sitting on the floor in our living room when all of a sudden Micah was on his back. Our little Malia was even more determined to grow up quickly, because she wanted to play with her big brother. Most babies start to roll over between four to seven months old. This is part of their gross motor skills development, and I highly encourage you to work with your baby and to give him "tummy time" each day on the floor beginning in his second month. This will help your baby strengthen his neck and back muscles that enable him to roll over and eventually stand up and walk.

If your baby can roll over during the night, she also has the motor skills to turn her head to breathe. So even though you put her to bed on her back, you don't need to worry about SIDS if she turns herself in her sleep. The American Academy of Pediatrics recommends using a firm mattress and avoiding all soft bedding, pillows, overheating or over-bundling.

Baby's First Words

One of the greatest gifts you can give your child is the gift of a good vocabulary and, later on, good communication skills. The more you talk to your baby, the quicker he will learn to talk to you. Everywhere I went with Micah—and I mean everywhere—I would name each item we saw. It didn't matter if we were grocery shopping or walking the trail behind our house; I named it. I carried Micah in the front pack facing out so he could see, and I talked to him. "That's an apple, a banana, a papaya and an orange," I'd say, pointing to each item. Or, "Look at the beautiful pink and yellow flowers," as we walked along the path.

As a parent, there will be times when you are not a good example, but each of us should try our best to speak words that will help and bless our children. Pleasant, joyful words will do wonders for your child's spirit, while unkind words will leave your child's soul wounded and crushed. Proverbs 16:24 says that kind words are like honey—sweet to the soul and healthy for the body. No matter what age your child is, I encourage you to speak words of life over him or her.

As my children grow up, I want them to avoid negative speech and foul language. My husband and I pray that God will enable us to be living examples of speaking praise and that which is uplifting. We want to live like the psalmist: "Let my mouth be filled with Your praise and with Your glory all the day" (Ps. 71:8).

Look at what Psalm 71:17 says: "God, You have taught me from my youth; and to this day I declare Your wondrous works." When we teach our children to speak "God's language," it becomes a lifelong blessing.

Nana's Journal

I was preparing to paint my living room and asked my daughter to come give me her opinion on colors.

As we were sitting in the living room with a pile of paint chips, my one-year-old granddaughter, attracted to all the pretty colors, picked up a chip and took her first solo walk across the room to show it to her mother.

Of course, we squealed with delight, hugged her and sent her back across the room for another paint chip.

I'll never forget the next 20 minutes, enjoying my first grandchild's first steps back and forth across my living room floor as she delivered paint chips to my daughter and me.

Carolyn Warren

Baby's First Steps

The day your baby first stands up is an exciting day. You know that soon your little bundle of joy will be taking her first steps. Malia had very strong little legs and loved to stand on my belly as early as four months old. She just loved it! So I'd let her do little baby squats to strengthen her muscles. Then, in December, we were fortunate to go visit my family and she took her first steps in Hawaii. It was so much fun to share those special moments with my parents.

Most babies will begin to walk between 9 and 12 months old, but others may wait until 16 to 17 months. Whether your baby is an early or late walker is not important. Either way, he or she will soon transition into a new world of independence.

Then again, maybe your sweet baby has special needs, like my friend's baby. It took her little guy much longer to crawl, talk and walk—and this is okay. He has his own timetable, and his parents rejoice in each milestone.

Jennifer Polimino & Carolyn Warren

I think there are some spiritual lessons we can learn by watching our little ones take their first steps. As Christians, we start off holding on to the hands of others—friends, Bible teachers, pastors. We are wobbly and unsure of our footing. As with a baby, it's cute at first; but we don't want our children to require handholding for balance when they are 10 years old. And that's the way it is with our Christian walk. We need to be eager to grow up, to delve into the Word of God daily for spiritual food and to strengthen our "spiritual legs" through prayer.

As parents, we pray for our children to grow strong and healthy; I also pray that we—as an entire family—continue to grow strong and healthy in the Lord. A good and challenging Scripture for parents to pray about is found in Galatians 5:16-17: "I say then: Walk in the Spirit, and you shall not fulfill the lust of the flesh. For the flesh lusts against the Spirit, and the Spirit against the flesh; these are contrary to one another, so that you do not do the things that you wish."

Parent's Prayer

Dear Father God,

I know You enjoy all of my baby's firsts as much as I do. I imagine You smiled the first day Jesus took His first stepsThank You so much for these special memories of my baby. They bring me such joy and happiness as I see my little one grow and flourish the way You designed. Help me never to compare my child to others, whether he/she is slower or more advanced; but instead, to be thankful for each milestone accomplished. Help me encourage my baby and to be faithful in prayer.

Lord, help both my spouse and me to walk daily in the Holy Spirit. Help us to fill our home with contentment and joy, with singing and praise. Keep us close to You so that we are not tempted by the pitfalls of evil. Keep us on the path of righteousness. And, Lord, show us where we need to grow spiritually. Apply Your Word to our lives and make us strong in You. Thank You for Your truth that is our daily spiritual guide. In Jesus' name, amen.

Scriptures for Thought and Meditation

This is the day the Lord has made; we will rejoice and be glad in it.
PSALM 118:24

*Light is sown for the righteous, and gladness for the upright
in heart. Rejoice in the Lord, you righteous, and give thanks at
the remembrance of His holy name.*
PSALM 97:11–12

Record your baby's firsts here:

- First smile _____.
- First bath _____.
- You rolled over all by yourself _____.
- Your first tooth _____.
- You slept through the night when you were _____.
- You waved bye-bye _____.
- You sat up without any help _____.
- You ate your first food when you were _____,
  and it was _____.
- You pulled yourself up _____.
- Your first haircut _____.
- You said "Dada" when _____.
- You said "Mama" when _____.
- You rode a toy with wheels _____.
- You walked all by yourself _____.
- Your first birthday was on _____.

Another memorable first was:

_____
_____
_____
_____
_____
_____
_____
_____
_____
_____
_____
_____
_____
_____
_____
_____
_____
_____
_____
_____
_____
_____

7

Baby's First Foods

Jennifer's Journal

Micah just turned six months old, and I can't believe he's already crawling around the house. He's discovered that he can get into some of the kitchen cabinets—the ones that don't have baby locks on them. He just loves the Tupperware cabinet. He enjoys playing with the containers—stacking them up and seeing them fall down.

This week he's ready to start eating real food. I've been researching the best first foods to feed him. I'm taking special care to avoid any highly allergenic foods because of my history with allergies. I think I'll wait until he's a bit older to introduce those to him. This week we will try bananas; next week will be avocados; and the third week will be sweet potatoes. I sure hope he likes the veggies, because in this family, he is going to be eating plenty of them!

The introduction to solid foods is quite a milestone for your little one. I know it was a big deal in our home. I recommend waiting until your baby is at least six months old, as does the American Academy of Pediatrics (APP).[1] If your baby is not quite six months old yet, don't feel like you need to rush her. There are telling signs that let you know when she needs more than only breast milk or formula. Answering a simple set of questions will help you decide when it's time for more substantial food.

When to Introduce Solid Foods

Here are seven indicators that your baby might be ready to eat real food (the first four indicate when a baby is physically ready, while the fifth through seventh are additional signs):

1. Has your baby doubled her birth weight?

2. Has your baby lost the tongue-thrust reflex? (Your baby automatically protrudes her tongue outward rather than back. Between four and six months this reflex gradually diminishes, and that spoon of bananas will actually be eaten and not spit out onto the floor!)

3. Does your baby have the ability to let you know she is full from a "meal" with signs such as turning her head away from the bottle or breast?

4. Can your baby sit up and hold up her head all by herself?

5. Does your baby show an interest in your food?

6. Is your baby waking up frequently in the middle of the night when a solid sleeping pattern had been established? (There are exceptions to this. For example, your baby might be teething at this age. When Micah was teething, he woke up throughout the night because he was uncomfortable, not because he was hungry.)

7. Is your baby going through a growth spurt? Growth spurts usually occur between 3–4 months of age, 6–7 months, and 9–10 months. During a growth spurt, your baby might want to nurse or feed all the time.

While it might seem like he is ready for solid foods, your baby may still need a little more time on the breast or the bottle.

Jennifer's Helpful Hints

If you and your baby are ready to move to solid food, I have a few recommendations that really helped my babies. First, make sure you introduce solid foods gradually. Give your baby a tiny taste, then wait and see what happens. You can use your breast milk or formula to dilute the first foods your baby tastes.

For example, let's say you picked a banana as your baby's first food. You can mix a little milk to thin it down and stir it into a creamier consistency. Your baby will probably eat only about one-half to one teaspoon initially. Don't ever force your baby to eat more than he or she wants, because studies show overfeeding might set the stage for childhood obesity.[2]

Make sure your hands are clean and use your finger as your baby's first spoon; this way you'll know if the food is too hot or too cold. And remember, proceed slowly by introducing only one solid food each week to see if your baby has an allergic reaction to something he's eating. (See the next chapter for more information on allergies.)

This is *not the time* to quit breast-feeding or feeding with formula. It is important to continue bottle- or breast-feeding for at least one year, using food only as a supplement, according to the Committee on Nutrition of the American Academy of Pediatrics.[3] I actually breast-fed both of my children until they were over two years old. At that point it was down to once a day and usually at night.

Best First Foods

After doing extensive research on the best foods to feed babies at various stages throughout the first year, I designed this handy reference chart. All of these foods can be steamed, boiled or microwaved and then blended, puréed or mashed until smooth. Bananas and avocados never need to be cooked first.

Birth to 6 months old	Breast milk or iron-fortified formula only
6 months	Bananas, avocados, pears, applesauce (no sugar added), sweet potatoes, squash, rice and barley cereal
7 to 9 months	Peaches, carrots, prunes, mashed potatoes, plums, pumpkin, green beans, oat cereal, poi (made from taro, a tropical tuber)
9 to 12 months	Spinach, rice cakes, egg yolks, plain whole milk, plain yogurt, rice cheese, poultry, lamb, veal

Some babies are allergic to a common "baby food." This is an important and crucial topic, so I've devoted an entire chapter to it. (Please see chapter 8.)

Making Your Own Baby Food

If you'd like to make your own baby food, it is easy, economical, environmentally friendly and healthier for your baby. I believe it is very important to try to use organic ingredients whenever possible to avoid pesticides. The first list will help you determine which fruits and vegetables have the most pesticide residue and are the most prudent to buy organic. You can lower your baby's pesticide intake substantially by buying organic or avoiding the 12 most contaminated fruits and vegetables—which are often called "the dirty dozen"—and feeding your baby the least contaminated produce. The second list shows the least contaminated produce and, therefore, those foods are not as critical to buy organic.

The Dirty Dozen (Buy Organic if Possible)

Apples	Spinach
Strawberries	Nectarines*
Celery	Blueberries**
Lettuce	Grapes*
Potatoes	Sweet Bell Peppers
Peaches	Kale/collard greens

Lowest in Pesticides (Buying Organic Optional)

Onions	Cabbage
Mangos	Watermelon
Avocados	Papayas
Pineapples	Cantaloupe**
Sweet Corn	Grapefruit
Asparagus	Sweet Potatoes
Eggplant	Mushrooms
Kiwi	Sweet peas

*   Imported
**   Domestic

My favorite kitchen gadget for making baby food when my children were babies was the Magic Bullet Blender. This tool made it so simple to purée just the right amount of food for my baby. Now there is also the Magic Baby Bullet, and it's BPA-free (non-toxic plastic). I sure wish that model had been available when my little ones were at this stage. If you don't want to invest in the Magic Baby Bullet, you can use a baby food masher, blender or food processor. They will work just as well.

One of my favorite tips is to prepare extra servings, then freeze the remainder in ice cube trays and cover with plastic wrap. That way, you'll have perfectly sized meals ready to go for times when you're too busy to make the food fresh.

On most Sunday afternoons, I spent an hour or two steaming and puréeing my little one's baby food. I froze each food separately in ice cube trays. (When my kids were older, I mixed two foods together, like banana-peach or sweet potato-broccoli.) The next day I popped them out of the ice cube trays and placed the little rectangles in air-tight freezer bags so they would stay fresher and fit better into my freezer. When I needed Micah's or Malia's meal, I simply took one out of the bag and returned the rest to the freezer. This saved me a lot of time in the long run.

Because my kids went almost everywhere with us, I always took one portion of these baby meals in a baggie with us. If we were at a restaurant or a friend's house, I asked for a bowl and a cup of hot water. I'd mash the food in the bowl and stir in a little hot water to warm it up—and *voila!*—we were all set. Or you could heat it in a microwave oven for a few seconds at a time. Just be careful to gauge the temperature before feeding your baby.

Daddy's Blog

It was good news to me when Micah began eating solid foods. I was itching to have some one-on-one time with my son, and sometimes that's hard to do in the early months when babies are so dependent on their mothers.

I remember the first time I decided to take Micah to lunch, just the two of us. He was not quite ready to eat the food at Hacienda Restaurant, so Jen packed his food to go, and I ate off the menu. I took out his little blue bowl of rice and mashed vegetables from the diaper bag and handed it to the waitress to warm up. It did not really matter what we were eating, it was more about the fact that I could take him out for extended periods of time without having to rush home so Jen could feed him.

I was so proud to have my son with me that day. I realize it may seem like an insignificant moment to some, but it meant a lot to me. It was an opportunity for me to say, "I am your dad;

I love you; you mean everything to me, and I want to spend time with you."

After we finished lunch, Micah accompanied me while I ran a few errands. We laughed, giggled and played games in the stores. It was a good day.

Feeding Your Baby While Traveling

Micah was on 36 flights during his first year! This was because Dan had many speaking engagements, and we were invited to come along. These trips gave our family the opportunity to see the new baby. When he began eating, I wanted to make sure I was prepared for these long flights. Of course, he was still nursing at six months old, so that made things easy when traveling. But soon he began to want more, so I made sure I brought along the right meals for him. I found that bananas are one of the easiest foods to travel with. Pears and plums were also great. I always took along a small cooler with my homemade baby food frozen in Ziploc baggies. I also brought along plastic forks, spoons and knives, a small plate or bowl and plenty of wipes.

Whether we were on the plane or in the car, I mashed up his food in the bowl and fed him with one of his little plastic spoons. I also brought along his Sippy cup and a fresh bottle of water. (The airlines allow moms with babies to bring these items onboard, and again I encourage you to bring the frozen portions you prepared to keep them fresh.)

When Micah was almost a year old, I discovered an awesome product: freeze-dried fruit. During takeoff and landing, if I couldn't get him to nurse, I put a tiny piece of this dehydrated fruit into his mouth to promote sucking. This, in turn, prevented his ears from hurting. I also gave him sips of water from his little cup to get him to swallow.

As I wrote this chapter, I wondered how long Mary nursed Jesus and what His first foods might have been. Historians tell us that in biblical times it was typical to breast-feed until age two to four.[4] (Those who were unable to breast-feed typically hired a wet nurse. Some royalty also hired wet nurses; so when Miriam (Moses' sister) offered to find a nurse for him after Pharaoh's daughter found him in a basket among the reeds alongside the river, it was not an unusual suggestion. [See Exodus 2:1-10.])

Jesus' first food might have been a mashed date or fig. Both fruits grew abundantly in Palestine. Other foods commonly grown in a family's own garden or in the village fields were melons, pumpkins, pomegranates, beans, lentils, peas, dandelions, cucumbers, lettuce and onions; so it's a good guess that Jesus enjoyed those foods as a child and during adulthood.

Figs and grapes were favorite fruits in Palestine, and grape juice was boiled to make a thick, sweet honey for bread. The sweet Cavendish banana most common in North America today was not cultivated until 1836, by a Jamaican, so we know that baby Jesus didn't enjoy our modern treat.[5] Wouldn't it be fun to someday ask Mary exactly what she fed Jesus?

Parent's Prayer

Dear Heavenly Father,

Thank You for this special milestone in my baby's life. I am so excited to introduce his first foods to him. You have provided us with such delicious food to eat on this earth, and I thank You for that.

Please help me, Lord, to know which foods will be best for my baby and provide his nutritional needs, and give me discernment to know when it is the right time to introduce them. As my child grows, help us to choose healthy, nutritious food and to avoid the temptation to eat junk food that is not good for the human body. I ask You to make me a good example of eating healthy and choosing wisely.

Keep us strong, both in body and spirit. Help me to internalize the "Scriptures for Thought and Meditation" so that I can apply them to my daily life and remember what You've said in Your Holy Word.

Thank You for Your grace and mercy, amen.

Scriptures for Thought and Meditation

Oh, taste and see that the Lord is good; blessed is the man who trusts in Him!
PSALM 34:8

And people should eat and drink and enjoy the fruits of their labor, for these are gifts from God.
ECCLESIASTES 3:13, NLT

Your first foods were:

_____

_____

_____

_____

_____

_____

_____

_____

_____

_____

Your reaction to them:

_____

_____

_____

_____

_____

_____

_____

_____

_____

_____

_____

_____

_____

_____

_____

_____

_____

_____

_____

_____

_____

_____

Notes

1. The American Academy of Pediatrics acknowledges that there are no strict age guidelines on introducing solid foods to your baby. However, "The AAP Section on Breastfeeding, American College of Obstetricians and Gynecologists, American Academy of Family Physicians, Academy of Breastfeeding Medicine, World Health Organization, United Nations Children's Fund, and many other health organizations recommend exclusive breastfeeding for the first 6 months of life. Exclusive breastfeeding is defined as an infant's consumption of human milk with no supplementation of any type (no water, no juice, no nonhuman milk, and no foods) except for vitamins, minerals, and medications. Exclusive breastfeeding has been shown to provide improved protection against many diseases and to increase the likelihood of continued breastfeeding for at least the first year of life." "Breastfeeding and the Use of Human Milk," *Pediatrics: Official Journal of the American Academy of Pediatrics.* http://aappolicy.aappublications.org/cgi/content/full/pediatrics;115/2/496 (accessed October 2011).
2. "Over-Feeding In Infancy Might Set the Stage for Childhood Obesity," Science Daily, May 17, 2005. http://www.sciencedaily.com/releases/2005/05/050517215812.htm. 11/2/2011 (accessed July 2012).
3. Ibid.
4. Ted Greiner, Ph.D., "History of Breastfeeding," December 25, 1998. http://global-breastfeeding.org/pdf/BF_history.pdf (accessed October 2011).
5. Peggy Trowbridge Filippone, "Banana History." http://homecooking.about.com/od/foodhistory/a/bananahistory.htm (accessed October 2011).

8

Allergies

Jennifer's Journal

Right now, Micah has just started his first foods. So far, so good. I've been worried that he will have some of the same allergies I have, but thank the Lord, he's okay so far. He loves to discover and taste every new food I give him, and he hasn't complained about anything yet. His favorites are bananas, avocados and pears.

I remember that while I was pregnant, I had severe allergies. This was a constant worry for me, so I prayed and prayed that Micah wouldn't have any allergies, and I believe God heard me. Thank You, Lord, in advance for giving me a child without any severe allergies.

The first few weeks after Sharon's baby arrived seemed to fly by. Busy with diapers, nursing, caring for a toddler and trying to keep up with the housework, Sharon barely had time to take a breath. Thank goodness she had family to help!

When their new baby was 13 days old, Ray and Sharon drove up to Wisconsin with their family. Everyone had a wonderful time, and they decided to stop and have ice cream on the way home. The baby was getting a little fussy, so Sharon decided to give her a little lick of the cold, creamy treat—just a tiny taste on the tip of her tongue. Almost instantly, her baby's face was covered with hives.

"Oh, my goodness, she must be allergic to it!" Sharon said. Soon, her new baby was crying with no end in sight. It took awhile to quiet her down; but finally, she nursed and fell asleep.

Months passed by, and the Christmas holidays arrived. Sharon made a lemon meringue pie, letting the older kids help in the kitchen. They were having a great time, licking the beaters and then kissing the newest member of their family. A few minutes later, their sweet baby's face was covered with hives in the shape of lips.

Ray and Sharon began to realize their new baby girl was born with severe allergies. They took her to a renowned pediatric allergist, Dr. E. Robbins Kimball. Tests revealed that she was allergic not only to dairy and eggs, but also to soy, wheat, chicken, beef, peanuts and fish. In addition, she was allergic to cats, dogs, horses and most other animals with dander or fur, and she had seasonal allergies as well.

Talk about having a difficult child to protect and raise! But that didn't discourage Sharon. She read every book she could find on allergies and how to handle them. In doing her research, she learned that nutrition and a healthy lifestyle play important roles in raising a child. She determined that she would help her little baby girl live a happy, healthy and full life, in spite of this challenge.

As a woman of faith, Sharon prayed in earnest for her baby. And you know what? God heard her prayers and opened up the right doors. He brought the right people into Sharon's life. Mary Lofton and Diane Kriz from La Leche League were a tremendous help and encouraged Sharon to continue to nurse her daughter as long as she could. They explained the benefits of nursing a child with allergies and why in many countries it's normal to breast-feed until the age of three or four. Sharon followed their advice, and her daughter continued to grow and flourish.

Yes, that little girl was me. Throughout the years, my allergies have been quite a challenge; but by the grace of God, He has healed me of many of them. I have been drawn to help others who also deal with allergies and other obstacles by teaching them proper nutrition and exercise, and the power of prayer.

With my lifelong history of allergies, I was cautious when I started feeding my children their first foods. I believe it's better to be safe than sorry when it comes to allergies and trying foods that are questionable during those first months and years. If there are allergies in your family, be cautious about introducing those foods to your baby, even if they are on the list of suggested first foods.

Nana's Journal

When my niece began having severe stomach pains on a daily basis, my brother and sister-in-law took her to the doctor. After running a thorough analysis, they could find nothing wrong. Even so, the daily pain continued. The doctor then referred her to a specialist 100 miles away.

As soon as I learned about this, I asked her about the stomach pain. Was it a severe nausea without throwing up? Did it last about 10 hours? Yes and yes.

By any chance, did the pain occur after eating a banana?

Come to think of it, she did have a banana in her lunch every day.

I told my niece about my own allergy to bananas and suggested she stop eating them to see what happened.

Boom—no banana, no more pain! The mystery was solved and no further medical intervention was required.

It's peculiar how sometimes an allergy doesn't show up for years, then all of a sudden it appears.

Carolyn Warren

Spotting a Potential Allergic Reaction

Notably, most allergic reactions occur within a few minutes to a few hours after consuming—or even touching—the item, as in my case, so be watchful after introducing a new food.

If your baby displays any of the following symptoms after eating, it might indicate a potential allergy or intolerance. Here are some common signs to look for: sudden, loose diarrhea stools and/or vomiting; sudden rashes on the skin and bottom; a runny nose; hives; irritability; bloating and/or gas after a new food; irregular breathing or other respiratory troubles after a new food; swelling of the face, lips and/or tongue; closure or tightening of the throat. (Intolerance to a food is not the same as an allergy to a food; and its symptoms typically involve trouble within the intestines.)

I have compiled a list of the most allergenic foods. I recommend that you avoid these when first beginning solid foods with your little one. Remember to *start slowly* and give your baby a *small amount*, maybe a quarter to half of a teaspoon, of one new food at a time. Wait four days or longer before introducing the next new food.

Avoid the Most Common Allergenic Foods

1. *Shellfish and crustaceans* are very highly allergenic foods. Therefore, it's best to wait until your baby is at least one to two years old. Or, avoid them altogether, as do people who subscribe to the Leviticus 11 diet.

2. *Honey* is not an allergen but it may cause botulism in infants under one year old.

3. *Peanuts and peanut butter:* Due to the highly allergenic factor, it is best to wait until baby is one to two years old. Some pediatricians recommend waiting until your child is seven years of age if nut allergies run in the family.

4. *Tree nuts* include almonds, Brazil nuts, cashews, chestnuts, filberts/hazelnuts, macadamia, pecans, pine nuts (pignoli), pistachios and walnuts. In some people, tree nuts cause a severe allergic reaction or pose a choking

hazard, so it's best to wait until your little one is at least a year old or even two years old. Again, some pediatricians recommend waiting until your child is seven years of age if these allergies run in the family.

5. *Citrus or acidic fruits* may cause an allergic reaction such as a rash or closing of the throat or digestive upset due to acidity, so it's best to introduce grapefruit, oranges, lemons, limes, pineapples and tomatoes after your baby's first year.

6. *Berries:* Raw strawberries, raspberries, blackberries are best after one year. (Blueberries and cranberries are *not* included in the list of berries to avoid for babies.)

7. *Corn* is a possible allergen and not very nutrient-rich, so it is best to wait until your baby is one year or older.

8. *Egg whites:* Most pediatricians say to wait until your baby is one year old.

9. *Dairy products/whole milk:* Many pediatricians recommend waiting until your baby is one year old to drink whole milk. Lactose and milk proteins may cause allergic reactions and may also cause tummy problems. Dairy products and cow's milk are hard to digest (yogurt and cheese are exceptions). Milk also hinders proper absorption of iron, and iron is crucial during the first year. Rice milk may be a better first choice for milk. I recommend the unsweetened version.

10. *Wheat, buckwheat and yeast:* Wait until your baby is over one year old due to wheat being a highly allergic food.

11. *Grapes* are not a high allergen but may pose a choking hazard; therefore, use extreme caution when offering your older infant or toddler grapes. It is advisable to wait until your baby is at least 10 to 12 months old, and take care to peel and cut the grape in little pieces, as I did for my kids.

12. *Coconut:* Children who are allergic to tree nuts might also be allergic to coconut.

13. Never use *salt, soy* or *sugar* when making your baby's food. Also avoid *cinnamon, mustard and chocolate.*

14. *Peas* are in the legume family, as are peanuts. However, a child might be allergic to peanuts but not to peas, and vice versa.

15. *Pork* carries parasites, worms and toxins. I do not recommend feeding your baby pork right now. Additionally, if you believe Leviticus 11:1-8 was given to us as a health code, then you may want to keep your family away from it entirely.

A surprising number of moms I've talked with tell me their child's physical delays were because of allergies to gluten, soy or eggs. If your baby is falling far behind in any area, and you suspect it might be due to an allergy, I encourage you to consult with a specialist about doing an allergy test.

Highly esteemed Dr. William Sears wrote, "Even the brain can be bothered by an allergic reaction. A new field of research interest, called 'brain allergy,' describes the behavioral reactions of the brain when it's bothered by certain foods."[1]

Environmental Allergies

There are other allergies to consider. Environmental allergies can play a large role to your child's discomfort. There are seasonal allergies like pollens; or your little one could be allergic to dust, mold, cigarette smoke, pets, grass, cosmetics such as hairspray, perfume, baby powder or strong-smelling deodorants, and dust mites, like I am. All of these listed affect me to this day. Once you figure out what the culprit is, try to avoid the allergen as much as possible. Keeping your home clean; getting rid of stuffed animals, carpet, pets and cosmetics can greatly improve your baby's overall health. If you live where the winter months bring a lot of cold, dry air, it's a good idea to use a clean warm-mist humidifier when your forced-air heat is on. Also, using a baby saline spray such as Simply Saline Baby Nasal Mist may also help your baby while your home is dry during those long, cold months.

Believe it or not, there is a child living in Minnesota who is allergic to the cold. That's right, the cold. When he goes from a warm to a cold environment, such as cold water or an air-conditioned room, he breaks out in hives.[2]

Please be aware that the information here is offered as a recommendation. Always talk with your pediatrician about any concerns you have and follow your doctor's advice.

I always believe in the power of prayer. I spent many hours praying for my children not to have the allergies I was born with. It was very difficult growing up with so many different allergies, and especially not being able to eat so many different foods. So far, Micah and Malia have very few allergies that we know of, and I thank God for that.

If your baby does have allergies, be encouraged with this: If they avoid the foods, animals or environmental allergens that affect them, they could very well grow out of their allergies. I just got tested at Kaiser a few weeks ago, and many of my former food allergies are now gone! Praise God—it took 42 years, but I am so happy that I don't have to be as careful about what I'm eating anymore. What a relief! I'm still praying for God to heal my dog allergy. The kids really want a puppy!

Parent's Prayer

Dear Lord,

You are a good and righteous God. I know how much You love me, and I know You love (baby's name). I ask that You keep my baby from serious sensitivity to allergens. But if she/he does have susceptibility to allergens, please show it to me today, Jesus, so I can help her/him avoid those dangers. Please give me the knowledge I need to minimize my baby's exposure to allergens. I want to protect and keep my baby safe, and I need Your help, Lord, to do that.

Please put the right doctor or person in our lives, who is skilled in this area of allergens, so that I can have help to make the right decisions for my baby. Give me the strength and the patience to feed the right foods and keep our home environment clean and healthy. Thank You, Jesus, for Your grace and mercy, amen.

Scriptures for Thought and Meditation

"For I will restore health to you and heal you of your wounds,"
says the Lord.
JEREMIAH 30:17

The Lord is my strength and song, and He has become my salvation; He is my God, and I will praise Him; my father's God, and I will exalt Him.
EXODUS 15:2

My Journal

My baby was allergic or sensitive to:

_____

_____

_____

_____

_____

_____

_____

_____

_____

_____

_____

_____

My baby had a reaction to _____
_____, and this is what happened:

_____
_____
_____
_____
_____
_____
_____
_____
_____
_____
_____
_____
_____
_____
_____
_____
_____
_____
_____
_____
_____
_____
_____
_____

Notes

1. "What Are Food Allergies?" AskDrSears, 2007. http://www.askdrsears.com/topics/feed ing-infants-toddlers/food-allergies/what-are-food-allergies (accessed November 2011).
2. Lori Obert, "Allergic to Cold," January 28, 2012. http://www.9news.com/rss/story. aspx?storyid=245567 (accessed February 2012).

9

Immunizations

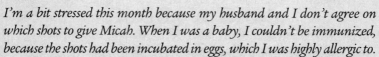

One of the biggest decisions you'll make for your baby is whether or not to get immunizations. To add to the complexity, you might choose some, but not all, immunizations. It's a major responsibility, one that is worth taking the time to look at all sides of the issue. First, let's take a look at what the experts say:[1]

- "Since there are currently 12 vaccines that are part of the routine childhood immunization schedule, parents have 12 separate decisions to make." (Dr. Robert W. Sears, M.D.)

- "Immunization is one of the most successful forms of preventative medicine and has helped to eradicate many formerly lethal diseases throughout the world. However, its continued success depends on strict maintenance of an immunization program in the community, and it is the responsibility of all parents to ensure that their children are fully protected." (Dr. Miriam Stoppard, M.D.)

- "We must seriously address what appears to be an obvious link between the epidemic of developmental delays, autoimmune diseases, and the increasing number of mandatory vaccines. Every parent should know . . . the positive and negative consequences of refusing that their children be vaccinated, and be made aware of how they go about getting exemptions." (Dr. Stephanie Cave, M.D.)

- "YOUR decision impacts OUR children." (Denise Fields and Ari Brown, M.D.)

I encourage you to read all sides of the issue before you make your decision. After all, this is *your* baby, not your doctor's baby, nor the Internet's baby. At the end of the day, you have to feel good about your decision. You have to go to bed at night knowing you made the best decision for your little one.

For me, it was important to make my choice coming from a place of knowledge and not of fear. Fear is not of God, and God does not want us to react out of fear:

For God has not given us a spirit of fear, but of power and of love and of a sound mind (2 Tim. 1:7).

You've heard the saying that "Knowledge is power." I pray that you use knowledge to cast out fear and then make a sound decision for your family.

Three Resources for Information on Immunizations and Vaccines

1. *The Children's Hospital of Philadelphia* has posted a web-page for their Vaccine Education Center. This resource is strongly in favor of immunizations. See www.chop.edu/service/vaccine-education-center/home.html.

2. *Loving-Attachment-Parenting.com* is a website set up by Christine Rieck and her husband, married for more than 20 years, and parents of a daughter, age 7, and a son, age 4, as of 2011. She quotes her baby's doctor, originally from Ireland, as saying, "If this were Ireland a hundred years ago, where sanitation and nutrition was very poor, I would call a person a fool to decline vaccination. But the situation is very different today." This website is about proceeding with caution and following a "selective schedule." See www.loving-attachment-parenting.com/baby-immunizations.html.

3. *WebMD* is comprised of articles written and approved by various medical professionals. It attempts to maintain a neutral tone and carries a disclaimer that it is not intended to replace your doctor's advice. See http://children.webmd.com/vaccines/tc/immunizations-overview.

Here are the 12 common immunizations:

1. Bacterial meningitis
2. Chickenpox
3. Diphtheria, tetanus and pertussis (also called whooping cough)
4. Influenza (also called flu)
5. Haemophilus influenzae type b disease (also called Hib disease)
6. Hepatitis A

7. Hepatitis B
8. Human papillomavirus (HPV)
9. Measles, mumps, rubella (MMR)
10. Pneumococcal disease
11. Polio
12. Rotavirus

Daddy's Blog

It's time to get shots for Micah. Jen does not want to immunize the kids, but I do. She has acquiesced to my wishes despite her own beliefs, and we are headed for the doctor's office. I have my usual stoic look on my face, as if to say, "I am sorry, but this must be done, and we'll all be just fine." After all, this was my father's approach.

Dr. Hall is very nice. He reassures Jennifer, answers all our questions and proceeds to give the shot to Micah. The needle goes into his leg and there is a bit of a delayed reaction, but the look on his little face, followed by the crying and tears, got to me more than I expected. Jennifer nursed Micah during the process and that seemed to calm him down pretty quickly; otherwise, I would have held him and hugged him.

Everything went well, but this was the first time in my life that I have experienced a pain I never felt before. I was suddenly aware of what my mother had said for all those years: "You feel the pain, as a parent, when your children are hurt." I thought this was just urban legend or "mother's talk," but I genuinely hurt when he hurt.

Pro and Con Arguments, Condensed

The primary argument against immunization is the possible side effects and/or bad reactions. Also, some people feel that since immunizations have done such an effective job of wiping out certain diseases, they are no longer (much) needed. There was also a scare that went viral concerning thimerosal-containing vaccines and autism. Parents read about a study in Britain that suggested a link between vaccines and autism and then, of course, reacted in horror and wanted to avoid the possibility of harming their child's brain.[2] A subsequent study proved that the so-called link between vaccinations and autism was false and baseless. Follow-up studies also showed no increase of autism in children who received vaccinations. Additionally, all routine childhood vaccines made for the U.S. now contain either no thimerosal or only trace amounts.[3] The primary argument for immunizations is that they do eradicate disease and the side effects are minimal and/or rare.

By now, you must be wondering what Dan and I decided to do. Let me first say that when you marry someone who has different beliefs than yours, you must learn to compromise. There are times when I don't feel that I should do something, but Dan feels the opposite. We spent many long nights talking this over and researched it until the wee hours of the morning, so we learned everything we could about immunizations. We finally made the best decision we could—one we felt would work for both of us.

I would have preferred fewer shots, if any, and I would have liked to wait a bit longer until Micah was older; but Dan wanted to get them all done right away. So we compromised. I had our son get one shot at a time unless it was impossible to separate them. We'd wait as long as we could so Micah could build up his immune system as much as possible. We did the same for Malia.

I wish I could say my kids never had a reaction, but Micah *did* have a bad reaction to two of his shots. The first time he was about six months old. We got home from the doctor, and he proceeded to get fussier and fussier as the afternoon wore on. By the evening, he wouldn't stop crying. I was exhausted and getting desperate, so I danced and danced with him in our living room for most of the night as I sang "How Great Is Our God" to him about a thousand times. I cried out to God, and He heard me. In the morning, Micah was better.

The second time Micah had a bad reaction was when he was 18 months old. He'd been given two shots on his chunky little leg. It swelled up with huge welts on the places his shots were administered. This lasted for days, and he complained that his leg hurt, and he ran a slight fever. I prayed over him and anointed him with oil. The welts and fever went away by day five. Again, he was fine. Praise God!

Basically, I came up with this plan of action for each and every time my kids get a shot:

1. First and foremost, I pray. I quote Scripture and pray over them that these shots will only help, and never hurt them in any way.

2. I nurse them (if they are still breast-feeding), while the shot is administered, to help relieve the pain. If they are not nursing, I hold them so they know they are not alone and that Mom (and Dad, if he is with us) is always there for them.

3. We ice the area, or our pedestrian administers a cold spray to make it bearable.

4. I make sure my children are feeling 100 percent healthy, with no runny noses, sore throats, allergies or fevers. If their immune system is at all compromised, it is not the time to get a shot.

All children's bodies are not the same, and it's impossible to know exactly how one child might react. No one can tell you what is best for your child. As parents, you do the research, pray and then follow your gut instincts.

As caring parents, we're often passionate about our decisions, but we must also respect other families as being equally passionate about their decisions for their children. The Bible does not tell us to immunize or not immunize. But Scripture does tell us not to judge one another (see Matt. 7:1), that gossip is perverse and separates close friends (see Prov. 16:28), and that we are not to disrespect a friend by calling her or him a fool or an idiot (see Matt. 5:22).

Now, if only there was an immunization against sin, wouldn't that be great? What if we could line up the whole family and get a shot that would wipe out all the temptation to be prideful, deceitful, selfish, hateful and pig-headed? How awesome that would be! God hasn't given us such a vaccine, but He has given us the next closest thing: His Holy Word. I pray that we, as parents—moms and dads alike—will do our best to immunize our precious children against spiritual darkness by taking a daily shot of the Word. As Psalm 119:11 says, "Your word I have hidden in my heart, that I might not sin against You."

Parent's Prayer

Dear God,

You designed my child's body and You know everything about him/her. Help me to make the right decision when it comes to immunizations and vaccines. Give me wisdom and give me peace from the Holy Spirit so that I know I'm making the correct choice.

Watch over and protect [child's name]. Never let any of the serious diseases attack his/her body. Keep my child well and healthy. I claim good health and protection over my family, in Jesus' name.

And, dear Lord, help me to live by Your Word. Give me a greater desire for Your Word. Help me carve out the time to read on a consistent basis. Increase my ability to memorize Scripture. Let me be a living example of hiding Your Word in my heart so that I do not sin against You. Guard my lips so that I do not gossip or put others down. I never want to be guilty of judging others.

Thank You for my precious child. Help me to be the very best mother/father that I can be. In Jesus' name, amen.

Jennifer Polimino & Carolyn Warren

Scriptures for Thought and Meditation

Don't be impressed with your own wisdom. Instead, fear the Lord and turn away from evil. Then you will have healing for your body and strength for your bones.
PROVERBS 3:7-8, NLT

It is to a man's honor to avoid strife, but every fool is quick to quarrel.
PROVERBS 20:3, NIV

My decision about immunizations, and how I arrived at that decision:

_____

_____

_____

_____

_____

_____

_____

_____

_____

_____

_____

_____

_____

_____

_____

_____

_____

_____

_____

_____

Two ways that I can make more time to read the Word of God and hide it in my heart:

_____

_____

_____

_____

_____

_____

_____

_____

_____

_____

_____

_____

_____

_____

_____

_____

_____

_____

_____

_____

_____

_____

_____

_____

_____

Notes

1. http://www.babyzone.com/baby/baby-health-and-safety/baby-immunizations/ (accessed October 2011).
2. "Immunizations: Topic Overview," November 12, 2010. http://children.webmd.com/vaccines/tc/immunizations-overview?page=2 (accessed October 2011).
3. Ibid.

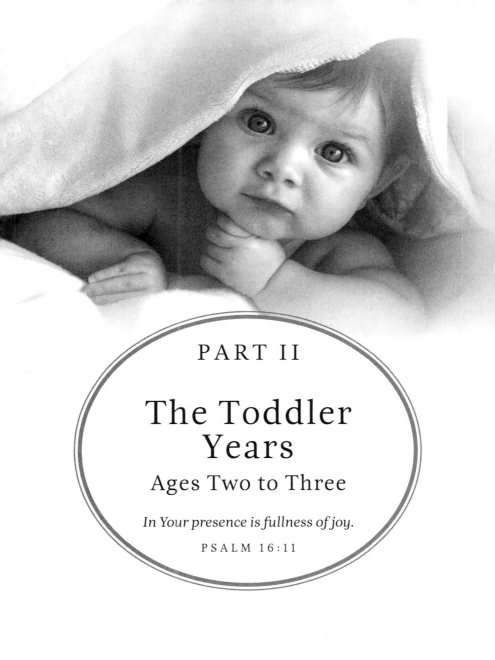

PART II

The Toddler Years

Ages Two to Three

In Your presence is fullness of joy.

PSALM 16:11

10

Toddler Behaviors and Setting Limits

Jennifer's Journal

What is going on? My dear, sweet little boy isn't listening to me anymore. He is now in his second year, and he's starting to tell me, "No!" I can't believe my innocent, happy boy is beginning to have meltdowns and is not listening to me. Where did my sweet baby go? Someone bring him back!

I remember when I was growing up; I was a bit older, but I spent many hours in my room for time-outs and then was grounded quite a bit when I was a teen. And yes, I got spanked a few times. But looking back, I deserved most of them. I'm trying to figure out what Micah will respond to and what is the proper "consequence" for this age. I'm reading so many books and there's so much contradictory information out there, it's really hard to decide.

When Micah was between two and three years old, he started to misbehave, and I didn't know what to do. I talked with my mom and with my younger sister who has four children, as well as with other mothers, about providing consequences for bad behavior, and specifically, whether or not to spank. It seemed like it was a pretty even split for and against spanking, with my family being mostly in favor. So the next time Micah did something wrong, I gave him a little spank on the bottom.

At first it seemed to work great; but after a few months went by, I could see something had changed in his normally sweet spirit. He became overtly aggressive when it was time for discipline. Soon the spankings did no good at all.

Looking back, I now believe this was mostly my fault because of the way I administered the spanking. I am a very emotional person, and I let my anger get the best of me at times.

When Micah was approaching age three, we took a trip to visit Dan's mom and stepdad in Utah. Micah's behavior had gotten so bad that we were finally at our wits' end. I was so embarrassed that Micah was being such a "little brat" while we were staying at Nana's house. I felt terrible, but no one had any good advice for me.

That's when I went online and found books written by medical doctors and psychologists who had conducted many years of research on thousands of children and their families—these were also Christian professionals who revered the Bible and loved kids. This wealth of information helped me understand what techniques could work at various times in my son's life. Soon I had my sweet little boy back again. Thank You, Lord!

What I discovered is that discipline styles pretty much boil down to four different philosophies.

Four Styles of Child Discipline

I believe that each family has the right and the responsibility to choose which discipline style (or combination of styles) works best for them. When it comes to kids, there is no "one size fits all." One child might be sensitive and quick to please and obey, while another child might be strong-willed—even within the same family. Therefore, it takes a lot of wisdom and prayer to discern what is best for each individual precious child. As I see it, here are the four styles.

Authoritarian
The parent is a strong authority figure, and the child *must* obey at all times. Discipline for misbehavior is immediate and consistent, and includes spanking. I was raised with this style, and I struggle not to repeat it with my own children. I believe that some of my problems during my teen years were due to this style of parenting. For example, I have to question why I was so afraid of getting my sister in trouble for taking me to her boyfriend's house that I did not tell my parents after I was molested by a group of boys there. I wish I'd gone to my parents for help, but I didn't want to tell them about the party for fear of getting my sister in trouble. (You can read more about my testimony in chapter 23.)

Communication
The key is to talk it out, the philosophy being "communication, not punishment." It sounds good, but have you ever tried reasoning with a two-year-old who is having a meltdown? This didn't always work for me.

Behavior Modification
Parents restructure the environment to influence negative behavior to move toward positive behavior. This didn't always make sense for me, either. For example, Micah could be screaming in the car, and there was no way for me to change his environment at the time.

Attachment Parenting
The parent is highly responsive and attentive. There is a strong emphasis on bonding, both physically and emotionally, to build proper boundaries. This is the style that works best for our family, especially when I am consistent. This style was conceived by Dr. Sears and Martha Sears, and is explained in *The Discipline Book*.

Nana's Journal

It seems to me we're living in a new age of entitlement.

Why do children think parents owe them a treat?

Why do kids think privileges are rights they deserve just for being alive?

Am I the only one who finds this new attitude troubling?

The other day I was in the grocery store when I heard a young girl say to her father, "Get these." She plopped a package into his cart.

"Hold on," he said. "Are you asking me or telling me?"

"Telling," she said.

"Put them back. That's not how you talk to me," the dad said, and he handed the package back.

His tone of voice was calm and yet it said he meant business. He pushed the cart ahead, without the item.

Carolyn Warren

Consistency Is Essential

Whatever style or combination of styles you choose, your child needs to know what to expect, where the boundaries are and what the consequences will be. Consistency is the key to any discipline program.

Any and all discipline programs will be ineffective if the parent is confusingly inconsistent. For example, it saddens me when I'm at the store and see a mom give in to buying a toy or candy after the child whines and fusses and begs. She has just taught her son that her "no" doesn't really mean no, and that he can change her parenting style through being disrespectful. On the other hand, I was impressed when I heard a mother say, "Don't ask me again. Asking over and over is not how I change my mind." She provided her son a good lesson about respect and saved herself a lot of emotional grief.

I've learned that getting connected and being an attached parent means staying sensitive to the child's needs right from the very start. It's important that as your child gets older you understand what is age-appropriate behavior. We can use humor wisely to promote cooperation in a toddler. Helping our child to respect authority by setting limits, providing structure and expecting obedience are important keys to success in raising a spiritually healthy child.

Nurturing a child's self-confidence, shaping his or her behavior, raising a moral and responsible child and simply talking and listening to the child are all part of attachment parenting.

We raise truly great kids by showing our children grace, just as our heavenly Father has done for us. In *Grace Based Parenting*, Dr. Tim Kimmel suggests that we apply God's love in four key areas of our children's lives: (1) We need to maintain a daily atmosphere of grace; (2) we focus on meeting their inner needs; (3) we build strong character; (4) we aim them toward true greatness rather than toward worldly success. In my opinion, this is also a wonderful approach to parenting.

In *Parenting with Love and Logic*, Foster Cline and Jim Fay write about how to teach our kids how to be motivated, confident and capable to solve their own problems. Their main premise is to give your child a task and allow her to make her own choices—whether good or bad—and allow her to fail while the cost of failure is still small.

The book *1-2-3 Magic for Christian Parents* by Thomas Phelan and Chis Webb worked well for us after we got back from that trip to Nana's. We were having a difficult time with Micah not listening and throwing temper tantrums. This simple counting approach worked wonders for our family and was age-appropriate for him. This approach helps control obnoxious behavior, encourages good behavior and strengthens the parent-child relationship. I encourage you to read more about this if your little one has begun some bad behaviors you'd like to correct.

If your children are like mine, using different approaches at different times in their lives works best. But first and foremost, spend time asking God to lead and guide you. He loves your little ones, and He will help you if you only ask.

Being a praying parent is the key to avoiding horrible pitfalls, such as reacting in anger. Jesus never lost His temper, never lost self-control. No matter what our children do, we must try to be an example of the love of Jesus Christ, never responding out of anger. I know that can be a challenge, and that's why we must keep ourselves in prayer and communion with our Lord throughout the day. Consequences for bad behavior are for the child's benefit, never an outlet for the parent to fly into a rage. If you struggle in this area, I suggest you seek help. Ask yourself if there is someone in your life or in your past whom you have not forgiven. Sometimes unresolved anger shows up at the wrong time and toward the wrong person—your child. I know this firsthand.

Here are two quotations I think are worthy of writing down and posting on the refrigerator or a mirror:

1. "When correcting a child, the goal is to apply light, not heat." (Woodrow Wilson)
2. "Praise loudly, blame softly." (Catherine the Great)

There were times when I had to leave my toddler screaming, go into my room and shut the door for a few minutes until I calmed down. One thing we can all agree on is that going too far with any discipline method crosses the line into child abuse, and that cannot be tolerated. If you feel yourself losing it, please reach out to someone for help immediately. Talk it out, take a break, play your favorite spiritual music and spend time waiting on the Lord.

Let's look at how Jesus honored children:

Assuredly I say to you, whoever does not receive the kingdom of God as a little child will by no means enter it (Luke 18:17).

Therefore whoever humbles himself as this little child is the greatest in the kingdom of heaven. Whoever receives one little child like this in My name receives Me" (Matt. 18:4-5).

The foundation of our parenting is to pray for God's help and then do our best at being proactive in setting up our children for success.

Recently, Dan and I drove to the Denver Rescue Mission to see what we could do as a family to help the homeless. As we ran out the door, I grabbed some sugar-free dried mango, natural pretzels, dry roasted nuts and plain popcorn. Actually, everywhere we go, I have healthy snacks and water with us in the car. It was lunchtime, but I knew this would hold the kids until we were finished at the shelter. In the car, I instructed the kids how I expected them to behave—to use good manners and show respect.

Once there, we spent two hours talking with Dan's friend Paul. We walked around the campus and held the kids when they needed a break. Dan carried Micah, even though he was six years old. When we finished touring, we sat down for another 30-minute talk, and I took pens and paper out of my purse so they had something to keep them busy.

The kids behaved wonderfully, and Paul even commented on how well they conducted themselves. The purpose of this story is to illustrate how parents can set up their children to succeed. We can teach our children how to be good testimonies of the Christian life.

Hunger, fatigue and boredom are common causes of a child's misbehavior. As parents, we want our children to act a certain way, so we need to help them be successful. Leaving home at one o'clock without lunch was not the best timing; but since circumstances worked out that way, I did the next best thing. To take care of hunger, I provided healthy snacks during the car ride. For fatigue, Dan and I carried them part of the way. And for boredom, I equipped my handbag with pens and paper. (For more information, see the next chapter about having a "Fun Bag" handy at all times.)

I try to be prepared wherever we go, whether it's to a restaurant, a friend's house or out shopping. Because of this, I am able to bring my children anywhere and not worry about their misbehaving or having a meltdown. That's not to say it has never happened; but I try to learn from my mistakes and then set them up for success the next time.

I've shared with you times when my children have behaved and when they have misbehaved, and I take both as opportunities to talk to Jesus. I thank Him when they are good listeners. When they are not, I turn to Him for His guidance.

When Malia was two years old, she sat in her stroller next to me for two hours without a peep while I had dental work done. The key was to get her prepared by telling her ahead of time what I expected. I also made sure she wasn't hungry and that she had something to keep her busy. Then I prayed.

Parent's Prayer

Lord Jesus,

I want to reaffirm my decision to dedicate my child to You. She [insert the appropriate pronoun throughout the prayer] is Your daughter first, then mine. I thank You for the privilege of bringing up my child.

I ask You to give her a spirit of kindness toward others. As she grows and learns to assert herself, also let her be aware that other people are equally important. Help her to be cognizant of their feelings too. Protect her from becoming a bully or a mean person. I ask for a godly child who has a heart open to You.

And, Lord, I realize that I need to do my part as well. Help me to be a loving parent—never angry—who models the fruit of the Spirit. But also help me not to be lax in bringing up my child in the way she should go. Give me wisdom in choosing the best methods of training. Help me to choose consequences for bad behavior that are effective and do not crush my child's spirit. Help me to be consistent, not lazy or selfish as a parent, and to take the time to exercise the consistency that's so important.

Lord Jesus, I rely on You for every area of my life, and that includes being a good parent. Let me, most of all, bring Your heavenly love to my precious daughter, as You would have me to do.

In Jesus' wonderful name I pray, amen.

Scriptures for Thought and Meditation

Train up a child in the way he should go, and when he is old
he will not depart from it.
P R O V E R B S   2 2 : 6

A fool vents all his feelings, but a wise man holds them back.
P R O V E R B S   2 9 : 1 1

My Journal

The method(s) I chose to discipline my child was/were:

_____
_____
_____
_____
_____
_____
_____
_____
_____
_____

The best way I found to help guide and shape you was to:

_____
_____
_____
_____
_____
_____
_____
_____
_____
_____
_____
_____

11

Playtime with Your Toddler

Since 1999, studies have tracked the effects of educational television on language development in toddlers. The results might surprise some parents. Experts found that watching television—including DVD players, computer programs, streaming video, and electronic tablets—actually *delayed* language development in toddlers.[1] And for children under two, the news is even worse. The American Academy of Pediatrics released a report on October 18, 2011, that says so-called educational media could "have potentially negative effects and no known positive effects for children younger than two years." They go on to say that "it should not be marketed as or presumed by parents to be educational."[2] Another study conducted by the University of California on 96 children, ages 12 months to 24 months, found that "infants do not appear to learn words from educational DVDs."[3] If you feel like I do, you don't appreciate deceptive marketing. I was one of the many moms who bought the Baby Einstein videos in hopes of giving our baby a head start.

As it turns out, the less time our children spend in front of a screen, the more time they have to enjoy play that actually is beneficial. Playtime provides an outlet for creative roughhouse development. And when we moms and dads join in the fun, it's good bonding time as well.

There are so many things you can do with your children that are fun, inexpensive, and that teach them so much more than a DVD ever could. In the following pages, I've listed ideas for you to use with your toddler to help her or him develop creativity and express artistic, musical and athletic abilities. I highly recommend going to garage sales, a dollar store or a thrift shop to find the materials you need. When my kids were at this age, money was pretty tight, and still is, so I don't spend a lot on crafts, athletic gear or musical instruments. And you know what I found out? It simply isn't necessary to spend a lot of money in order to have tons of fun with your kids. (Even though these ideas are in a chapter for toddlers, older children will enjoy them as well. Micah is now six, and he still loves to do them all.)

Daddy's Blog

I, like many men, have often thought about what it would be like to raise a son. Countless times I have visualized the sports

I would teach him to play, the days in the park together and lots of moments just horsing around.

If I ask Micah what he wants to play, 9 times of 10, he'll say, "I want to roughhouse, Daddy."

I am always up for roughhousing, but Jennifer is not such a big fan. I have tried explaining to her why boys and their dads need to roughhouse, but she doesn't quite get it. Let's face it, she's not a guy and probably won't ever know why beating on each other is good for dads and their boys.

Boys have a ton of energy and aggression. They need to release that. Even though I may have spent 10 to 14 hours working that day, I will still lie down in the middle of the floor so my son can beat on his dad. Sometimes I am not sure if I even understand it. I just know it makes us happy.

24 Ideas for Creative, Stimulating and Valuable Play Time

Creativity for a Rainy Day

1. Noah's Ark
This is a favorite with both of my kids. Cover some sturdy chairs with a big sheet to construct an "ark." I've used hair clips or hair claws to keep the sheet from slipping. Gather *all* the stuffed animals in the house, some snacks and a flashlight. Pick the person who wants to be Noah, then crawl inside the ark and have fun talking about what you thought it was like on the ark, what foods the animals ate, how dark it must have been at night, and so on.

2. Lava Lamp or Wave Bottle
These objects are fascinating for little ones to make and play with. Fill a clean, empty bottle one third full with water. Add a few drops of food color, beads, glitter, sequins and tiny seashells (whatever you have available), and then fill the rest of the bottle with baby oil. Glue the cap on securely and enjoy the waves!

3. Make a Tie Snake

My little guy came home with one of these from preschool recently. First, grab an old tie that you can't stand your husband to ever wear again. Then stuff it full of cotton batting from an old pillow. Sew the tie closed and let your toddler glue on button eyes and a little felt tongue (he can cut it out by himself with child-safe scissors). Fabric glue works well, or I like to use a hot glue gun; but if you use a glue gun, make sure *you* attach the eyes and mouth so your sweetie doesn't get burned. Let your child beautify and dress up his snake any way he'd like with markers or by gluing on more decorations.

4. Animal Toss

No work involved here, just fun! Gather your child's favorite stuffed animals or stuffed balls and a laundry basket for the toss. Let her stand fairly close to see how her aim is, and then as she gets better, have her back up two steps after each round.

Tons of Fun for a Snowy Day

5. Snow Painting

Fill spray bottles with water. (You can get cheap bottles from a dollar store or wash empty spray bottles from cosmetics or household cleaners.) Add 8 to 10 drops of food color to each bottle (or more, depending on the size of the bottle). Now is a good time to show your children how mixing blue and red makes purple, mixing yellow and red makes orange, and so on. When the "paint" bottles are done, bundle up the kids and let them decorate the yard. It's so much fun, and you'll have the most beautiful yard on the block!

6. Build a Snow Panda

Malia's favorite animals are panda bears. So instead of always building a snowman, we now build snow pandas. I shape a large oval snowball for the body and a smaller, round one for its head. I found that a black to-go container works well for cutting out black eyes, a nose and a mouth; but you could cut them out from

black construction paper too. We also add black gloves for the arms and black socks for the feet. It sure makes her smile! You can build just about any favorite animal!

7. Save Ice from Heaven

While growing up in Hawaii, I always ate shave ice, or as you say here on the mainland, snow cones. A truly good-tasting shave ice is made of superfine ice; so when we get a large amount of snow here in Colorado, and it's fresh and clean, we scoop it off of our outdoor table and bring it in the house in giant bowls. We make giant 12- to 18-inch tall volcanoes. I then pour fruit juice all over them.

"It so delicious, Mommy!" my three-year old says.

"God makes the best shave ice ever!" I always tell her.

For a healthy topping, please don't use anything with food coloring or sugar. Fruit juice is best. I recommend Mighty Mango by Naked Juice (their other flavors are tasty as well), grape juice or fresh-squeezed orange juice.

8. Treasure Hunt

Gather together some of your child's hard plastic toys that won't get damaged when wet. Carefully hide them in the snow. Then tell your child how many treasures he has waiting for him buried in the snow. Dress him appropriately and give him a small shovel to dig with. If you hid them well, you may have up to a half-hour of free time to sit and read while watching him find the treasures.

Your Little Artist

9. Box Train

Cut the tops off of three medium-sized boxes (tissue, cereal or any small box will do). Take a five-foot rope and cut it into four pieces—the first should be two feet long and the other three pieces one foot long. Make two holes in the sides of the boxes, in the middle on opposite sides of each other. Tie the rope into one hole and use a popsicle stick to anchor it in there so the rope won't slip out. Attach all three boxes together using this same method and save the longest rope for the pull cord. Let your toddler paint or decorate boxes with pens or crayons. Fill the boxes with his favorite toys and he'll pull it around the house for days!

10. Feather Painting

All you need are paper, feathers and washable paint. Give your child a few feathers and some washable paint, and then let her make you a work of art. Frame the best one.

11. Sheet Painting

Similar to the snow painting, fill small spray bottles with water, adding eight to ten drops of food color to each one (more for larger bottles). Hang an old white sheet on a chair or barbecue outside. Let them squirt the beautiful colors all over the sheet, creating their own original designs. Your kids will love to see the masterpiece they've created. (The sheets usually wash out in hot water with no staining.)

12. Sewing Boxes

I came up with this one the other day while I was trying to write this chapter and Malia was getting restless. First, cut a 14- to 16-inch square from a medium-sized cardboard box. Then draw the face of your child's favorite animal on the cardboard. You guessed it: Malia chose a panda. Using a paper hole punch or a screwdriver, poke large holes around the outline of the animal's face. Next, cut a 25-inch to 30-inch length of yarn. At one end, wrap or roll a toothpick with Scotch tape to form a "needle." Tie a large knot on the other end to prevent the yarn from going all the way through the hole. Now you can show your little one how to "sew" the animal. Starting on the backside, thread the needle through a hole and draw the yarn up. Then poke the needle through the next hole and pull through, thereby sewing around the animal's face. It's fun to see the project take shape, and it's good hand-eye coordination as well.

Your Budding Musician

13. TP Kazoo
Save those empty toilet paper tubes for this project. Punch a hole in the tube near the middle of the tube. Completely cover one end with a 4" x 4" piece of newspaper and secure it with a rubber band. Let your child decorate the "kazoo" with markers or crayons. Blow the open side of the tube for a really fun sound.

14. Dancing with God
All you need for this is some great Christian music and to get off the sofa. We have our favorites on our iPod, like Chris Tomlin's "How Great Is Our God" World Version; "Move" by Mercy Me; or "Trust in Jesus" by Third Day. We crank up the volume and dance around, singing praises to God. Even Daddy joins in the fun.

15. Pots and Pans Marching Band
When Micah was almost two, he just loved to play with all the pots and pans. One day, we decided to make our own marching band. We each got a wooden spoon and a frying pan and marched around the house singing, "Marching, marching, marching around the house." We giggled and went on banging, switching to large plastic spoons and spatulas to create sound variations. We had a wonderful time together!

16. Shake It Up
Fill a washed coffee can with dried lentils, beans or corn. Glue the cover on and let your princess decorate her new instrument. She will have tons of fun shaking it all around the house. How long

you can handle the noise is another question; so, weather permitting, encourage her to play with it in the yard.

P.E. for your Toddler

17. Mommy, May I?

I got this idea from Carolyn and found that it can be a lifesaver at bedtime. Have your kids stand at a "start line" in the living room.

Mommy says: "(Child's name), please take one giant step and one bunny hop toward your bed."

Child answers: "Mommy, may I?"

Mommy says: "Yes, you may," and the child takes the steps.

Mommy then gives the next child the instructions, or the next instructions to a single child. You can use kangaroo jumps, bunny hops, ballerina twirls, baby steps and other creative movements to create fun for your child.

If your child forgets to say "Mommy, may I," she must start all over at the beginning. You'll have your children giggling their way into bed instead of whining and crying.

18. Rope Balance

All you need is a long rope. Lay it out on the grass or on your floor in your living room in zigzags, curves and loops. Your little one must "balance" her way to the end of the rope and back. A special kiss and hug at the end is the prize! This is a great idea to keep them busy while you're folding laundry on the couch.

19. Dodge Ball

We love to play dodge ball in our house, using a soft ball so no one gets hurt. Let your toddler run around while you try to hit him gently. We like to turn on our local Christian station, K-Love, as well. You can also switch places, and let him try to hit you. You'll fall over giggling in no time.

20. Beanbag Toss

You can buy beanbags or make your own. To make beanbags, locate colorful or cute fabric and cut into six-inch squares. Then sew the edges closed except for a one-inch hole. Fill the squares with dried beans, lentils or uncooked corn kernels, and then sew the hole closed. Next, get a *big* box and cut out large holes. Mark each hole with 10 points, 20 points, 30 points, and so on, so that your child can learn how to add points and keep score. Let your child try to toss the beanbag into the holes.

Fun While Traveling

21. Sticker Art

On your next trip, bring along colorful craft paper and a good variety of stickers. Let your child choose colored paper and create a work of art with the stickers. I know we left a few stickers on the plane window last time we did this, but it sure looked cute.

22. Snack Guessing Game

Twist a variety of small snacks into different-colored tissue paper. Have your child guess what each snack is. Or simply throw all the snacks into a brown paper bag and have your child stick his hand in and, without looking, guess what the snack is before he takes it out of the bag. Only healthy treats, please!

23. Paper Bag Puppets

Gather small paper bags, craft paper, glue stick and child-safe plastic scissors. Help your little one cut shapes out of the craft paper for the eyes, nose, ears and mouth of her favorite animal. Then let her paste them on the paper bag. You can use markers as well for face details. Have fun making different voices for each puppet. Tell stories about your upcoming vacation, and talk about how excited you are.

24. Wrap It Up!

The week before you get on a plane or head out for a long car ride, pick up several small toys, new crayons, coloring books and stickers at the dollar store. Wrap each little gift for your toddler to unwrap as the flight or long ride gets underway. I did this for Micah when he was two-and-a-half and on his way to Hawaii. Whenever the flight was delayed or he was about to lose it, I'd pop out another present, and his smile would quickly return. Because you know what is in each one, you gauge which gift gets opened and at what time. It was a lifesaver for me since Malia was just born and nursed quite a bit. The gifts sure made Micah feel special.

One of the joys of being a parent is seeing the happiness of our children as they play. It's fun to watch them and to hear the funny things they sometimes come up with. I can't help but think that's the way our heavenly Father sees us. God takes no joy in seeing us sad, sorrowful, downtrodden or depressed. In fact, joy is one of the major themes in the Bible, and He delights in our joy: "He will yet fill your mouth with laughter, and your lips with rejoicing" (Job 8:21).

God Himself will fill our mouths with laughter—I love that, and that's the kind of happiness I want in my family.

One of my hobbies is painting. I painted both of my children's rooms, with some help from my friends for Malia's room. As they got older, I let the kids help me. We just added another backhoe pay-loader and cement truck to Micah's walls, and a giant mommy and baby panda to Malia's jungle-themed room. They just love to help out and feel special with their custom-designed rooms.

Expressing creativity is one of the ways I like to play. When I read the first chapter of Genesis about God creating the moon and stars, all the different plants and animals, and the grand finale—a man and a woman—I notice that after each day, God sat back, surveyed His handiwork and saw that it was good.

Genesis 1:27 tells us we are created in the image of God. To me, that says we are made to be creative, artistic, musical and athletic—for the glory and pleasure of our Creator. What a fun God we have!

Parent's Prayer

Dear Lord Jesus,
   Thank You for the delight and joy You have given us. Thank You for the happiness—and yes, the fun playtimes—we can share with our children.

Help us not to forget the joy of being a child. Help us to take time out of our schedules to play and never become "too busy" for our son/daughter. Remind us of the value of family time and bonding together as a family, for we know You have ordained the family.

Bless our family with a good sense of humor. Bless us with creativity and athletic ability. Help us discover what our son/daughter is good at and encourage those talents. Use whatever talents You have given us for Your glory. And bless us with the deep-down gladness that comes from being a child of God. Let us never forget to be glad and to praise You.

In Jesus' wonderful name, amen.

Scriptures for Thought and Meditation

Praise Him with the sound of the trumpet; praise Him with the lute and harp! Praise Him with the timbrel and dance; praise Him with stringed instruments and flutes! Praise Him with loud cymbals; praise Him with clashing cymbals!
PSALM 150:3-5

A joyful heart is good medicine.
PROVERBS 17:22, ESV

Your favorite play activities at age two:

_____
_____
_____
_____
_____
_____
_____

_____
_____
_____
_____
_____
_____
_____
_____
_____

At age three:

_____
_____
_____
_____
_____
_____
_____
_____
_____
_____
_____
_____
_____
_____
_____

Notes

1. Virginia B. Hargrove, "Study Confirms that Turning Off TV Protects Baby's Brain!" http://www.pregnancy.org/blog/study-confirms-turning-tv-protects-babys-brain (accessed November 2011).
2. Ibid.
3. Bettye Miller, "Infants Do Not Appear to Learn Words from Educational DVDs," March 1, 2010. http://www.eurekalert.org/pub_releases/2010-03/jaaj-idn022510.php (accessed January 2011).

12

Manners, Please

Maura Graber, who has been teaching manners to children and adults for 15 years and is the director of the R.S.V.P. Institute of Etiquette, says this on the importance of children learning good manners: "Historically, mothers taught manners to children, but the whole structure of the American family has changed tremendously, and not just by 'moms' going to work. In a lot of cases now, there may not be a mother . . . in the home at all. The basic principles of having good manners are simply unselfishness and consideration."[1]

Most parents dream of having polite and courteous children. Saying, "Please, thank you, and I forgive you" is the foundation to developing a Christlike spirit. Do you know that your two-year-old can be a testimony of your Christlike home?

Having well-behaved children takes effort. For some children, manners come quite easily. For others, it may be a daily battle (but one worth fighting).

From the day our babies can watch and listen, they observe how we treat others. By the time they are toddlers, they're experts at imitating us. They notice when we treat people kindly and give them grace. They also notice if we are rude to a solicitor at the front door or to a driver cutting us off in traffic. The first example begins with our own family members, right at home.

I shouldn't be surprised when I see a toddler, or even an older child, disrespecting his or her parents or another adult without the parent doing something about it. And yet, the indifference to rudeness is something I can't get used to.

I have learned that children go through phases, and there will be seasons when a child may be ever so polite, and then the next day he or she will act like a completely different little person. I've gone through this with Micah twice, and I try my best to nip it in the bud. The first time was when he was about three years old at Nana's house (as I wrote in chapter 10); the second time was when he was five, approaching six. The consequences of being given a time-out or losing his favorite toys seem to work the best for him.

Malia, now three years old, has mastered the art of polite talk. I am so proud of her and love it when she says, "No, thank you, Mommy," or "Oh, yes, please." But there have been a few days when she left her manners at home. Looking back now, I think we were having a stressful week, and she wasn't feeling her best; but that is still no excuse for rudeness.

We were at Kohl's department store two days ago when Malia spotted a panda shirt she really wanted. Both of my children know I don't buy them anything if they beg and whine for it. I had actually found the shirt and hidden it in the cart to put in her stocking for Christmas, but she soon discovered it. She just wouldn't stop asking for it. I told her to please stop it or I would put it back on the shelf; she decided to have a meltdown instead. So I left the store with a crying toddler in tow—but with no shirt! The key, I believe, is not to give in when your children misbehave or are impolite or rude. Stick to your guns and follow through with their consequences. I had told her, "No shirt if you keep asking for it," and I meant it.

If I had bought her that shirt, it would have taught her that bad behavior pays off and I don't mean what I say. So I had to follow through.

Demonstrating courtesy, politeness or good manners simply means showing kindness and thoughtfulness—acting in consideration for others. Jesus is our best example of that. He treated others with compassion and grace. Scripture tells us that as a boy, "Jesus increased in wisdom and stature, and in favor with God and men" (Luke 2:52).

The apostle Peter, by inspiration of the Holy Spirit, wrote, "Finally, all of you be of one mind, having compassion for one another; love as brothers, be tenderhearted, be courteous" (1 Pet. 3:8). That's pretty clear to me.

So how can we effectively teach our children to use good manners? Here are four principles to keep in mind.

Teaching Toddlers Good Manners

1. Start young.
2. Be encouraging.
3. Set a good example.
4. Don't quit. It's a never-ending process.

A checklist can be helpful in keeping you on track and ever mindful of how you want your children to behave so that they, like Jesus, grow in favor with God and man. I created a "good manners" checklist to hand out when I speak to groups, but it's also a good reminder for myself—a report card of sorts. I hope you find it helpful as well.

Jennifer's Good Manners Checklist for Toddlers

You might want to read through this list with your children and lead them in doing a self-assessment.

☐ *Does my child use the words "please" and "thank you" to show respect and appreciation?* A great tip for your toddler is to use stuffed animals or puppets to practice saying "thank you" and "please." Kids love to play games, so if you can teach them the "magic words" by playing, it's a fun and effective way to teach them to use their polite words. It's also nice to teach your child to receive compliments courteously. If someone praises your child, teach him or her to be gracious and say "thank you" rather than put himself/herself down or point out flaws. I struggled with this for years because I had low self-esteem; but I want my children to learn to accept a compliment that is deserved.

☐ *Does my child say, "I'm sorry" and "I forgive you"?* These are some of the most powerful words you can teach your children. If they can master the art of saying, "I'm sorry" and "I forgive you," they will build better relationships wherever they go. Many adults have a difficult time admitting they were wrong because they never learned to do so when they were young. Saying you're sorry to your children when you've yelled at them for no good reason or taken out your anger on them is truly the way to teach them that we all make mistakes and no one is perfect. Teaching them to forgive is just as powerful.

☐ *Does my child avoid interrupting others?* We struggle a lot with this one in our family. We are not a very quiet family, and we all have a lot to say. I know that growing up in a large family was partially the reason that I tend to interrupt sometimes. We had to yell over each other just to be heard. It's a terrible habit I have been working on to break. My kids sometimes interrupt, as well, and they know the best way to get my attention is to say "excuse me" nicely and then wait while they place their hand on my arm or leg. I then put my hand on top of theirs so they know I've heard them. I try not to leave them waiting too long since they asked so nicely; and at that age, they can't wait forever. Be sensitive about giving your child your full attention when you are done speaking so that you reinforce the positive behavior of waiting his/her turn. Just make sure your child doesn't use a loud "excuse me" as a means to rudely interrupt.

❑ *Does my child use good table manners?* This applies both at home and when dining out. It might be self-explanatory for some, but other kids may need some time to master these tips. First, encourage them to place their napkin on their lap when they sit down for a meal. Let them know it's polite to eat with a fork or spoon (or chopsticks, if those are the eating utensils), to chew with their mouth closed and not to stuff their mouths with too much food at once. Encourage them to ask for something to be passed to them and not lean across the table. There are many times when my kids don't love what I make for dinner, but they are not allowed to speak rudely of the food I serve. If they don't want to eat something, they don't have to, but then that will be their next meal. For breakfast not so long ago, my son had turkey meatloaf, honey glazed carrots and broccoli, while the rest of the family had fresh banana-granola pancakes—all because he had not yet eaten his dinner from the night before. We never force our children to eat, but I will not make multiple dinners at once. It's also courteous to wait until everyone at the table is seated and ready to eat. And remember: eat slowly, ask to be excused from the dinner table and thank the chef for preparing the meal.

❑ *Is my child truthful?* Proverbs 12:22 says, "Lying lips are an abomination to the LORD, but those who deal truthfully are His delight." Teaching our children not to lie is very important—God even made it one of the Ten Commandments.

Micah is at the age where he is starting to lie about little things; for example, this week he took a piece of candy off of the gingerbread houses we made and ate it. When I asked him about it, he denied it at first. But then I got the "Are you gonna be mad if I tell you the truth?" sentence. I always tell my kids that if they tell me the truth, I will not be mad. They may have to face the consequences, but what I really want them to know is that they can trust me and come and talk about it, no matter what it is. Start now with the little stuff, because when they are teens, it will be far worse if they are not truthful.

☐ *Does my child clean up after himself or herself?* Cleaning up after oneself shows responsibility, and I believe that the younger you start your children to help clean up their messes, the easier it will be on you as a mother in addition to teaching them personal responsibility. Whether we are at home or at a friend's house, I always try to lead by example and instruct my children to pick up after themselves. Toddlers will respond to a fun tune, so I like to sing, "Clean up, clean up, everybody clean up." Taking on this responsibility also builds their self-esteem.

☐ *Does my child obey parents, teachers and elders?* Listening carefully to adults and being courteous and respectful toward people in positions of authority is very important. God instructs children to honor their parents (see Exod. 20:12) and promises them long life if they obey. I was with a group of kids one day when one child was very disrespectful to me. I let it slide a few times, but finally I had had enough. I put the child in a time-out away from our group. I never want my children to behave like that toward an adult, so I teach them to respect their elders.

☐ *Does my child show good sportsmanship?* After playing a game (sports, cards, board game), no matter the outcome, I try to teach my children to be pleasant. If Micah or Malia wins, I tell him/her to not gloat or show off, but to be kind. If they lose, they are not allowed to sulk or get mad, but to be a good sport and tell the other players "good game" or speak well of them. Micah is having a hard time with this lately, but he's learning that we won't play with him if he's a poor sport.

❑ *No name-calling! Does my child obey this rule?* In our family, name-calling is not allowed if it hurts the other person's feelings. Even if it's in "fun," name-calling can hurt. My husband has always come up with pet names for all of us, but I can see lately that some of the names are bothering Malia. Even though they are sweet and endearing names, I've told Dan he needs to stop them.

❑ *Does my child greet people in a courteous manner?* When someone comes over to our house, I teach my children to wait to open the door until either Dan or I are with them, for safety reasons. I then want them to greet our guests so they feel welcome. The minimum requirement is saying "hello" or "hi" and maybe a handshake, if appropriate. In Hawaii, I grew up in a culture where you hug and kiss everyone on the cheek as a greeting, and we still do this with close family and friends. You may also want to let your toddler offer food or beverages to the guests, as a courtesy.

❑ *Does my child hold the door open for others?* I believe that teaching children to be aware of others is an important concept. I tell my children whenever they walk through a door to make sure to hold it open for the next person so that it doesn't hit them in the face. They should also thank the person who holds the door open for them.

❑ *Does my child share?* Sharing can be hard at any age, but especially for toddlers! It's a process that takes time. At first, they learn to take turns with a toy, then to share the toy. If you start young and help your child learn that sharing is both fun and a way to make someone feel good, they will, hopefully, learn that sharing is a way of life.

❑ *Does my child use proper hygiene?* Hygiene is for both manners and cleanliness: Use a tissue when wiping your nose; cover your mouth when you cough or sneeze; and *always* wash your hands after using the restroom. Putting the toilet seat down and remembering to flush (we're still working on this one!) are important as well. And if you burp or toot, please say, "Excuse me."

❑ *Is my child kind to others?* Jesus said to do unto others as you would have them do unto you (see Matt. 7:12). Everyday manners could look like this: Do not cut in line; do not stare; do not point; apologize if you bump into someone; wait your turn. Simple to us adults, but these may take practice for your toddler.

Nana's Journal

My son and daughter are only 18 months apart. During one season of time, they fell into using bad manners at the dinner table. No amount of correction or reprimand worked to prevent this bad behavior.

Since I don't believe in depriving young children of the food their bodies need, I didn't want to send them away from the dining room. I just wanted them to stop the purposely loud burping and other offensive acts they seemed to find so funny.

Then I had an idea. I purchased a small votive candle for each family member. That evening, I dimmed the lights and lit a "personal candle" by each of our plates. I explained that having a candle was a privilege, and if they used bad manners, they had to blow out their personal candle.

Voila! You never saw such a fast transformation in good table manners. No more bad behavior, and everyone was happy—especially this mama.

Carolyn Warren

So how did your child do on the quiz? You might want to write down any points they need to work on, or make a reward chart for improved behavior. List the things they need to work on, and each time they do a good job, award a star. After 20 or 30 stars, they earn their reward. It could be a special outing to the park or a small toy from a dollar store.

As parents, we are the CEOs of raising well-mannered sons and daughters. We're the ones in charge of teaching them the rules of etiquette, such as to take your hat off in church; keep your knees together when you wear a dress; wipe your shoes at the door; take off your shoes in someone else's home; watch your language; make eye contact when talking with someone; and dress properly for the occasion. It's a job that never ends, but it's a job that brings satisfaction and great reward.

Showing good manners is very important to me, and I feel pleased when someone comments on how polite my children are. Like the other day at Costco, Malia said "thank you" to a nice lady who retrieved a book she had dropped on the floor. I was just a few feet away, picking out avocados, but I was watching the situation unfold. The lady turned and complimented me on "what a polite little lady" I had. It made me smile, and I'm sure Malia's "thank you" made Jesus smile too.

Parent's Prayer

Dear Heavenly Father,
I know that You designed us in Your image and that You are a Gentleman. You are patient and kind to us and show us respect

and grace. Please help me to teach my child to be courteous to others. Help me show [child's name] how to be respectful and polite by my examples.

If there is an area I need to work on, please bring it to my attention, right now, Father, and guide me in the right way to correct it. I know there are times when I am tired or angry with someone else and my manners go right out the door, so please help me to be a better example for [child's name] to follow tomorrow and every day.

Thank You, Jesus, for being a wonderful example for us, and for Your forgiveness and grace.

In Your gracious name I pray, amen.

Scriptures for Thought and Meditation

Finally, all of you be of one mind, having compassion for one another; love as brothers, be tenderhearted, be courteous.
1 PETER 3:8

Save me, O Lord, from lying lips and from deceitful tongues.
PSALM 120:2, NIV

You are so polite in these areas:

_____

_____

_____

_____

_____

_____

_____

_____

_____

_____
_____
_____
_____
_____
_____
_____
_____

We are still working on being polite in these areas:

_____
_____
_____
_____
_____
_____
_____
_____
_____
_____
_____
_____
_____
_____
_____
_____
_____

Note
1. "How Does One Learn Good Manners?" http://www.essortment.com/one-learn-good-manners-36768.html (accessed November 11).

13

Spiritual Training

The apostle John wrote, "I have no greater joy than to hear that my children walk in truth" (3 John 1:4). When I see Micah and Malia learning God's truth and coming to know their heavenly Father's love, I have no greater joy as a mother.

God's Word tells us, "Direct your children onto the right path, and when they are older, they will not leave it" (Prov. 22:6, *NLT*). We are to guide our children when they are young so that when they're older, they are already well onto the right path and won't stray off into spiritual danger. This is both a command and a promise.

My parents taught me the truth; but as a teenager, I fell far away from God. When I was older, I came back to the Lord. I know those prayers my mom prayed were heard by our heavenly Father.

According to Deuteronomy 11:19, we are to teach our children in God's ways both morning and night, at home and on the road—in other words, all the time and everywhere we go.

Dan and I want our children to realize that the Holy Spirit is always right there with them, and He will never leave them. When my kids are afraid, I encourage them to pray for courage and to use their authority, praying, "in Jesus' name." I want them to understand that they are children of the Most High God (and I pray that sooner than later they will ask Jesus to be their Savior and Lord). In the meantime, we tell them that no matter what they do, Jesus will always love them and forgive them, just like He does everyone who comes to Him and becomes His child.

So I encourage you to talk to your children daily about Jesus and to set a good example by spending time with Him each and every day. I've found that the closer I get to Jesus, the better mom I am, the more patience I have and the happier I am.

How can you, as a godly parent, direct your children onto the right spiritual path while they are still tots?

Five Ways to Lay a Solid Spiritual Foundation for Your Children

1. Family Prayer
Prayer comes first. If you read our first book, *Praying Through Your Pregnancy*, you've been praying for your child since conception. What a firm foundation you've already laid! Now, when your little one is old enough to talk in sentences, he or she can join in simple prayers at mealtime, before bed and throughout the day.

Eating dinner together is a must, and that is one of the times when you can pray together as a family, holding hands and thanking God for your many blessings. We encouraged our children at a very young age to join in on prayer. We never force our children to pray, but we give everyone the opportunity to lead in a prayer or to simply thank God for one thing, which is a great place to start.

2. Family Devotions
Reading Scripture and discussing how you can apply it to your lives is for everyone. You don't need to have a degree in theology to read the Bible with your children and talk about who their heavenly Father is and how He takes care of us.

When Micah was 18 months old, his Uncle Danny, my bother, came for a visit. Danny helped Micah memorize his first Scripture, Proverbs 3:5: "Trust in the LORD with all your heart." I knew right then that we were off to a good start.

Malia learned her first Bible verses at a young age as well. How I taught my children was quite simple. While they sat and enjoyed their meals at the table, I wrote out the Scriptures and drew little pictures about what the verse was saying; or I'd act it out. They loved seeing mommy act silly, and I believe this greatly impacted how they learned God's Word at such a young age.

3. Music and Song
Simple tunes like "The B-I-B-L-E" and "Jesus Loves Me" help cement a solid foundation right from the start. Micah and Malia absolutely love to sing and to worship God through song. As I mentioned previously, my children watch very little TV, but one thing I do allow them to watch once in a while are the live-action song DVDs by Cedarmont Kids. We have the Platinum Bible Collection, which are beautifully done videos of children singing popular Bible songs. Both of my children just love these DVDs. I also found some great CDs called "102 Full-length Bible Songs" for the car. Everywhere we go, Micah, Malia and I sing our hearts out to God. It makes driving in the car so much more fun.

4. Church Worship
Toddlers are not "too young" to be a part of praise and worship. In *Praying Through Your Pregnancy*, I cited scientific studies that

show babies hear even before they are born. Therefore, I see no reason to exclude them at this age. There is immeasurable value in having your little ones beside you while you stand in the congregation, worshiping God. They need to see their parents as part of the congregation, lifting their voices in song and prayer, because they learn by observation. Paul wrote, "Imitate me, just as I also imitate Christ" (1 Cor. 11:1). Our children cannot follow our example of participating in church if they don't have an opportunity to observe it.

5. Kids' Ministry Class

If you are fortunate to be part of a church with a strong kids' ministry program, that is a blessing. I chose not to put my kids into the church nursery when they were little, especially when they were still nursing. I loved having them with Dan and me, worshiping and praising God as a family. But as they got older, we switched churches and now attend Cherry Hills Christian where there is a wonderful children's ministry. The kids love their Sunday School classes, but at times they are allowed to sit with us in church as long as they sing nicely and then sit quietly and color during the message.

Mommy Devotions

I have a special message for the moms who feel frustrated that their husbands do not lead in a time of family devotions. You are not alone.

Thousands of mothers—including single moms, moms whose husbands are serving in the military overseas, and moms in other circumstances where the father is not involved—are doing "Mommy Devotions" on their own. If this is you, I encourage you to take hold of your God-given authority and rise up to be the spiritual leader of your children.

Salome is an example of a strong Christian mother during Jesus' time. She was the mother of two of the men Jesus chose to be His disciples: James and John. What an honor! Salome was definitely a follower of Jesus (Scripture refers to her presence at the crucifixion—see Matthew 27:55-56 and Mark 15:40-41), and I believe she was the spiritual leader in her house, for three reasons:

1. No mention is made of the father, so it seems that, for whatever reason, the mother was in the leadership role.

2. Salome went to Jesus and asked if her sons could sit next to Him in heaven. Now that's what I call an ambitious mother who was looking out for her sons' best interests! Even though there was a much deeper spiritual context in this conversation (Jesus' emphasis on the importance of being a servant rather than seeking status), Jesus explained that the decision was in the hands of His Father. I have to give her credit though for taking the initiative and having the courage to ask (see Matt. 20:21-23).

3. She handed down a rich spiritual legacy. It was her son John that Jesus entrusted His own mother to when He was on the Cross of Calvary. And many Bible scholars believe her other son, James, was the first apostle to be martyred for the Christian faith.

Even though the Bible tells us much more about John and James than it does about their mother, Salome is a good example of spiritual leadership.

Interview with Katy Cerny
Ministry Leader at International House Of Prayer (IHOP)

JP: *How does IHOP support families with children?*
Katy Cerny: IHOP supports families with children of all ages. When you embrace this lifestyle as a family, you are able to bring your children to the 24/7 prayer room. We teach kids how to pray, worship and engage. We also have a prayer room specifically for the

children to lead once a week. It's called Malachi 4:6. It is an amazing place filled with the Holy Spirit. Children who are less than two years old will stand up and pray, and the Holy Spirit comes upon them. Kids of all ages are welcome.

JP: *What does IHOP teach the children?*

Katy Cerny: The heart of our vision here at IHOP is to intentionally develop opportunities for children of all ages to be equipped to understand the call of 24/7 prayer and worship; to heal the sick through the laying on of hands; to prophesy, preach, and teach; to give from their hearts to the poor; and to evangelize the lost. We want to provide our children with opportunities to express and grow in their gifts as musicians, singers and prayer leaders. IHOP teaches children the same things they teach the adults, but on their level—prayer, worship and fasting (for a child, fasting is not from food but from TV, games, media, music.)

Also, IHOP teaches children about serving, as this can be considered fasting of your time; and fasting from money or giving of your money instead of buying something else with it, which can also be considered fasting.

JP: *Could you share a healing story with us today?*

Katy Cerny: A seventh-grade girl on my basketball team was sick, so I asked her if I could pray for her, and she said yes. I started out praying that her body would align and that no sickness would be in her body. I pleaded the blood of Jesus over her and proclaimed that "by His stripes, she was healed" (see Isa. 53:5). I prayed in tongues for a little while and then felt like I was supposed to ask her if she needed to forgive anyone. I explained why she needed to forgive, if there was someone the Lord highlighted to her. She said, yes, she did need to forgive; and right there, she forgave some individuals who had committed wrongs against her.

After she did, I prayed for her again and led her in adoration of the Lord. I asked her to say a prayer of thanks for what the Lord is doing. After worshiping the Lord for about five minutes, she was completely healed. Praise the Lord!

Then, as she followed the lead of the Holy Spirit, healing came to her friend. It was key that she listened to the Lord's voice as she prayed. He led her to highlight the need of forgiveness in her friend's heart. Lack of forgiveness can sometimes hold back the healing, as it says in James 5:16: "Confess your sins to each other and pray for each other so that you may be healed" (*NLT*). The Bible is clear that forgiveness is a command, not an option. Forgiveness means releasing and turning them (the offender) over to God, and it frees our hearts to receive healing as well.

Jesus told us, "For if you forgive men their trespasses, your heavenly Father will also forgive you. But if you do not forgive men their trespasses, neither will your Father forgive your trespasses" (Matt. 6:14-15).

Unbelief and fear also hold back healing. In Mark 6:5-6, we read that Jesus marveled at the unbelief of the people in His hometown. It says that because of this unbelief, "He could do no mighty work there, except that He laid His hands on a few sick people and healed them." We need to separate ourselves from fear and unbelief, "For God has not given us a spirit of fear, but of power and of love and of a sound mind" (2 Tim. 1:7).

Paul wrote, "But we have the mind of Christ" (1 Cor. 2:16).

JP: *Is there online support for parents who cannot travel to Kansas?*

Katy Cerny: Yes. You can visit us at http://www.ihop. org/cec/. Also go to http://www.ihop.org/about/ and you can be part of the prayer and worship Web stream. It's on 24/7.

JP: *What is the children's prayer and signs and wonders movement?*

Katy Cerny: These are our Signs and Wonders Camps where children are trained and released to be wholeheartedly devoted to God. Our vision is to see one million children radically committed to Jesus, walking in the power of the Holy Spirit, and moving in signs and wonders. At our camps, we teach children to know and love God; walk in the power of the Holy Spirit; love, respect, obey and honor their parents; and to live by the Word of God. We also encourage our children to encounter God in worship and prayer. They also learn about hearing the voice of God and healing the sick. Children who are ages 6 to 7 may attend the day camps, and ages 8 to 12 can sleep over. To see if there are camps near you, log on to http://www.ihop.org/cec/signs-wonders-camps/.

Parent's Prayer

Heavenly Father,

Thank You for ordaining that young children, and even infants, have been called to praise You. And thank You for entrusting my child/children into my care.

I pray that I will be a living example of a life that is devoted to You. I don't want to get stuck in a meaningless routine or be overly legalistic about following a schedule or a checklist; but I do want to use every tool You have given to lead my children on the path to You. Help me to direct, guide, and train up my child in the ways of the Lord. Help me to teach them Your Word and to memorize it so they might not sin against You. Enable me to teach them how to pray in a real way. Let us talk to You from our hearts, going beyond memorized prayers. Help me bring spiritual music into our home and automobile. Help me teach my child how to praise and worship You.

Lord Jesus, I ask You for wisdom and guidance. Nothing is more important than the spiritual welfare of my children. Stop me when I am about to do something wrong, and help me to be a good example—always honest, patient and kind. Help me to guard the words of my mouth, especially when my children are present.

I dedicate our family again to You. Help us live our lives for Your glory.

In Jesus' name, amen.

Scriptures for Thought and Meditation

Out of the mouth of babes and nursing infants You have perfected praise.
MATTHEW 21:16 (QUOTED FROM PSALM 8:2)

Fix these words of mine in your hearts and minds; tie them as symbols on your hands and bind them on your foreheads. Teach them to your children, talking about them when you sit at home and when you walk along the road, when you lie down and when you get up.
DEUTERONOMY 11:18-19, NIV

My Journal

Little ones can say the cutest prayers to God. If you'd like to record a prayer your child said, here is a space to do that. Or you may choose to record your own prayer for your child to read when he or she is older.

_____

_____

_____

_____

_____

_____

_____

_____

14

Help for Your Sick Child

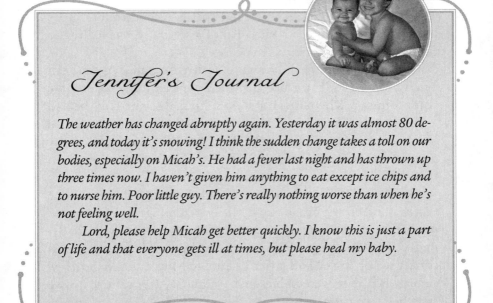

Jennifer's Journal

The weather has changed abruptly again. Yesterday it was almost 80 de-grees, and today it's snowing! I think the sudden change takes a toll on our bodies, especially on Micah's. He had a fever last night and has thrown up three times now. I haven't given him anything to eat except ice chips and to nurse him. Poor little guy. There's really nothing worse than when he's not feeling well.

Lord, please help Micah get better quickly. I know this is just a part of life and that everyone gets ill at times, but please heal my baby.

I had just returned from taping my Christian testimony with *Focus on the Family* and begun work on writing this chapter when Micah came down with the flu. It only lasted a day, but then Malia got it too.

The first thing I do for my children when they're sick is to pray over them and anoint them with oil. I base this on James 5:14: "Is anyone among you sick? Let him call for the elders of the church, and let them pray over him, anointing him with oil in the name of the Lord"; and Mark 6:13: "And they cast out many demons, and anointed with oil many who were sick, and healed them." I take these Scripture verses to heart, and I believe that Jesus has the power to heal our children when they are sick, and that we need to tap into this power.

Because I grew up with severe allergies, my parents conducted an extensive and thorough research on using natural remedies. They not only studied allergy relief, but also relief from all types of sicknesses for all of us kids. That background has led me to become a big fan of natural remedies.

I am thankful my children are healthy overall. Yet, they can catch a cold or the flu, especially when their immune systems are compromised. When Micah started school, it seemed like he had a cold every week. It was so tiring and frustrating, and it seemed like he was never going to get better. As a mother, I wanted my child to feel better right away, but I also didn't want to give him too much medication that might harm him.

In 2011, Johnson & Johnson took Infants Tylenol off the market; and after a broad recall, the Food and Drug Administration urged consumers to stop using liquid Tylenol, Motrin, Benadryl and Zyrtec medicines for children and infants. I was concerned because I had given Tylenol to Micah and Malia a few times when they were babies and toddlers. After that scare, we switched to natural remedies to help my kids feel better; and by using these natural remedies, their symptoms were much less severe and lasted for a shorter time.

Nowadays when your child has a stuffy nose, tummy ache or sore throat, doctors say that natural remedies are often the best way to help your child feel better, and that makes me very happy as a mother. Even the well-loved Dr. Oz is a big fan of age-old home remedies—treatments that have been tested over hundreds of years and rarely have any side effects. They don't cost much, and many times, you'll already have what you need in your own kitchen.

I've come up with a list of natural remedies for you to consider the next time your little one gets sick or hurt. In addition to using these remedies, make sure your child always drinks plenty of water, eats a healthy balanced diet and gets enough sleep—all are key to keeping the immune system healthy. Also, give your child a good whole-food multivitamin supplement each day, and make sure he or she has clean hands, using plain soap and water. (It is no longer recommended to use an antibiotic soap because it can breed resistant bacteria.)

12 Natural Remedies to Use When Your Baby, Toddler or Child Is Sick

I hope you will try these the next time your little one needs relief from pain.

1. Upset Tummy

When my guys have an upset tummy, I often give them chamomile or peppermint tea. It relaxes the intestinal muscles and has a calming effect. I steep the tea bag for four to five minutes, let it cool a bit and then add in a little honey. (Honey is okay if your child is at least 12 months old.)

A highly effective herbal supplement is Little Tummy's Gripe Water by Little Remedies. It contains sodium, ginger and fennel extract, which also help relieve gas and stomach discomfort from colic and hiccups.

2. Sore Throat

My kids really love lemon juice and honey. The lemon helps to dry up congestion and the honey provides a soothing coating to the throat. In fact, a recent study found that one spoonful of honey eased kids' coughs even more effectively than regular cough medicine.[1] Our favorite is Organic Ohia Lehua honey (bigisland bees.com), or you can try buckwheat honey; both seem to soothe a sore throat. Simply mix together one tablespoon each of lemon juice and honey, microwave for 10 to 20 seconds until warm (not hot), and have your child swallow the mixture one teaspoon at a time. Caution: Honey is not safe for babies under one year.

If your child is old enough, you can have him try gargling with salt and baking soda (half a teaspoon of each in a cup of warm water). At our house, we also like herbal teas, such as slippery elm, cherry bark or licorice (not anise), which are also soothing. There is even a tea called "Throat Coat" for kids by Traditional Medicinals, which we all love. If your child prefers something cold on the throat, try making 100 percent fruit juice popsicles or homemade "ice cream." (See chapter 15 for my recipe.)

Nana's Journal

Most of us have become so accustomed to the convenience of email that we're out of the habit of sending handwritten notes through the postal service. The best thing about that is that it's made old-fashioned greeting cards all the more special.

When one of my grandchildren is sick with the flu, I like to send him or her some mail. If it's one of the older children, I'll handprint a letter and add a few stickers. If it's for a younger child who isn't yet reading, I'll send a cute greeting card or a hand-drawn picture.

Receiving a special envelope in the mailbox really brightens up their day. And I've received some delightful letters in return.

Carolyn Warren

3. Headache
Many times when your little one gets the flu, he may also get a headache. The best thing you can do is to wrap a soft, flexible gel ice pack, or a bag of frozen peas or corn in a dishtowel, and place it on his

head. (Never place the ice pack directly on his skin because it may burn him.) This will soothe your child's head pain without using Tylenol.

4. Colds and Congestion

Do you know what to do if your child comes home with a miserable cold? Well, my children *love* to get a big teaspoon of "caramel," as I call it. It looks like caramel to me, and all you do is mix one teaspoon of honey (raw honey is best) and a quarter-teaspoon of cinnamon. I give it to them twice a day for three to four days for best results. We like to mix it in our oatmeal, drizzle it on homemade pancakes or make a "tea" with it. It's important to take this at the first sign of a cold.

If your child is not asthmatic, you can also use a humidifier or steam from a hot shower to help ease congestion. (Changes in humidity can cause bronchospasms for asthmatic children.) If your child has nasal congestion, try having him sleep on his side as much as possible. This helps keep mucus from slipping down the throat. Or you might want to use a cool mist vaporizer to ease discomfort; you can add a few drops of menthol, eucalyptus or peppermint to the water for added healing.

Again, make sure you are giving your child lots of water or juice, or anything the child will drink. If he or she is not thirsty, try a homemade sugar-free fruit juice popsicle. I also love to freeze Recharge by R. W. Knudsen Family (It's a natural hydration drink with electrolytes and no sugar. You can find it at your natural grocer.) It can help your child combat dehydration.

Don't forget the benefit of homemade chicken soup—it's still a mainstay. Keep it simple and all natural. I make mine with antibiotic and hormone-free chicken, carrots, celery, onions, garlic, chicken or vegetable bouillon and bay leaves. Salt and pepper to taste. It's light, nutritious and tastes good to young appetites. We like to add brown rice or rice noodles as well.

5. Bug Bites and Bee Stings

If your child gets a bug bite or a bee sting, first remove the stinger by scraping it off with a credit card. Next, apply a cold ice pack wrapped in cloth for a few minutes while you prepare a baking soda paste.

This helps to stop the itching better than any store-bought product. The alkaline baking soda helps counteract the acidic swelling. Simply mix one teaspoon of baking soda with just enough water to make a thick paste, then smear it on the bites and allow to dry.

Remember, the two greatest risks from most insect stings are allergic reaction (which in some individuals can be fatal) and infection (more common and less serious). Seek medical help immediately if either allergic reaction or infection occurs.

6. Swimmer's Ear

Micah started swimming at a very young age and had earaches, or swimmer's ear, once in a while. This painful inflammation of the outer ear traps liquid and, possibly, bacteria inside. In the case of infection, your pediatrician will probably prescribe antibiotic drops. But for mild cases, you can try evaporating the trapped water by standing a foot away from your child and aiming the dryer—on the warm (not hot) setting—at his ear. You can also try Similasan Earache Relief or NutriBiotic Ear Drops.

I know some parents are accustomed to making the trip to the doctor for the "pink medicine" (amoxicillin); but nowadays, many doctors are getting away from that for ear infections unless you will be traveling on a plane soon.

7. Fever

When your child gets a fever, it's not always a bad thing. God designed our bodies to naturally kill bacteria and viruses. In most children, fevers less than 102 degrees usually don't require treatment unless the child is very uncomfortable. Call the pediatrician if your child's temperature is higher than 102 degrees. However, infants younger than three months old are at a higher risk; and therefore, it is recommend to immediately call your doctor or go to the emergency room for any temperature of 100.4 degrees or greater.

I believe it's okay to just let a mild fever work in toddlers and older children. If your child is feeling pretty warm, you can try a lukewarm bath or take the blankets off and use just a light sheet to cover him or her with. Make sure he or she is drinking lots of cool water.

8. Leg, Foot or Neck Pain

Instead of buying a heat wrap, you can use one of the rice bags we talked about making for the "bean bag toss" in chapter 11. You can also use these bags for tummy, leg, foot or neck pain. Simply fill a sock or piece of cotton or flannel fabric with uncooked rice. Tie it shut with yarn or string or sew the ends together. Heat the rice bag for one minute (or longer as needed) in the microwave or until warm. *Make sure it is not too hot!* Then place it wherever your child has pain. When it cools off, microwave it again and reuse.

If heat isn't helping, you can try the frozen corn or peas, or the soft cook gel ice packs. Do what feels best for your child.

9. Toddler Constipation

There may be a time when your little one gets backed up. There are a variety of things that can cause kids to get constipated, such as a change in routine, an illness or medication; but the most common cause is usually diet or dehydration.

If a child has constipation, the first thing I would suggest is increasing his water intake. As soon as he wakes up, I'd give him a glass of warm water to drink. Next I'd give him psyllium husks, which is a natural fiber supplement that can be added to a glass of water or 100 percent fruit juice. Then make sure your child is drinking plenty of water throughout the day.

I would proceed to give my child fresh fruit for breakfast. We always say, "Fruit first!" at our house, and they both love it. You can give your child prunes, raisins or figs to eat throughout the day, as these are all great in helping to get the bowels moving. Also, my chiropractor, Dr. Michael Pesta, recommends Ready! Set! Go! by Ortho Molecular. It has most of the ingredients listed above in liquid form and works for my kids within 24 hours.

10. Nosebleeds

Cayenne pepper helps blood clot and has been used medicinally in cultures around the world, says pediatrician Lillian Beard, MD, author of *Salt in Your Sock and Other Tried-and-True Home Remedies*. Neither my children nor myself have ever had a major nosebleed. But

Dr. Beard recommends keeping your child's head upright, sitting tall and pinching her nostrils together for several minutes. Then sprinkle a pinch of ground cayenne pepper on a moistened cotton swab and dab inside the nose on the area of the bleeding. "It seems like it might sting; but, surprisingly, it doesn't," says Dr. Beard.

11. Carsickness or Nausea

I'm lucky that both of my children love eating fresh ginger. I started giving it to them around the age of two when we were having sushi for a special occasion. My mom taught me that ginger helps stop the stomach contractions that tell your brain that you feel nauseated or have motion sickness. Ginger is safe for children age two and older to drink as a tea made of one teaspoon of shredded fresh ginger for each four ounces of boiling water. Allow the drink to steep for four to five minutes, and then you can add a bit of honey to make it taste better. After it has cooled, have your child drink it half an hour before getting into the car if she is prone to motion sickness or her tummy feels upset.

12. Croup

When Micah was a baby, he got croup a couple of times. Croup is a viral inflammation that results in difficulty breathing accompanied by a barking cough. It was very scary for me as a new mom. I found that nursing him and keeping him hydrated was the first important thing to do. Next, I placed a humidifier in our room to help him breathe normally.

Fill the humidifier with plain water and a pinch of salt. Don't forget to empty, clean and completely dry out the humidifier between each use to prevent mold growth. Over-the-counter cough and cold medicines are not helpful for treating croup. If your infant has croup, a trip outside into cold air, for a few minutes, might help as well.

I pray that these natural measures will go a long way toward assuring that your child stays as healthy as possible. As you read the Scriptures and pray, ask the Lord to give you wisdom and speed the healing process. I believe we need to use common sense, the resources we have available and also tap into God's healing power. Here are some of my favorite words from the Bible to inspire faith.

Seven Favorite Bible Verses on Healing

I am the LORD who heals you.
EXODUS 15:26

He sent His word and healed them.
PSALM 107:20

"For I will restore health to you and heal you of your wounds," says the LORD.
JEREMIAH 30:17

Go your way; and as you have believed, so let it be done for you.
MATTHEW 8:13

He Himself took our infirmities and bore our sicknesses.
MATTHEW 8:17 (QUOTING ISAIAH 53:4)

These signs will follow those who believe: In My name they will cast out demons; they will speak with new tongues . . . they will lay hands on the sick, and they will recover.
MARK 16:17-18

The prayer of faith will save the sick, and the Lord will raise him up. And if he has committed sins, he will be forgiven. Confess your trespasses to one another, and pray for one another, that you may be healed.
JAMES 5:15-16

Scripture records the story of a man named Jairus whose only daughter became seriously ill (see Luke 8:40-56). Jairus spent all he had for medical intervention, but her condition worsened. Desperate, Jairus traveled to Jesus in order to plead for help.

Jesus consented to Jairus's request, but it was a long trip on foot, and Jesus was interrupted and delayed by others who needed healing. While they were on their way, one of Jairus's house servants ran to them and said, "It's too late. Your daughter has died." I can only imagine how this news must have devastated this loving father.

But Jesus said, "Don't worry; she is only sleeping and will be made well. All you have to do is have faith and believe."

At this point, Jairus was faced with a choice. He could choose to cancel Jesus' trip because his daughter had died; or he could choose to believe his daughter would rise again. He chose to believe, and on they went.

When they arrived at Jairus's residence, Jesus pushed past the mourners and the skeptics and took the girl by the hand and said, "Child, get up!"

Miraculously, the daughter opened her eyes and rose up, completely well and healthy. I love this story. It is an account of unstoppable faith, of parents standing in for their child, of doubters in the midst, of a miraculous restoration, and then of happiness mixed with surprise. There are some good lessons for us parents here.

Parent's Prayer

Dear Lord,

I ask You to watch over and protect my child from illness. I speak good health and safety over [child's name] now, in Jesus' name.

Help me to be a good, responsible parent. Help me in times of difficulty to make the right choices. Lead me and give me wisdom.

In times of sickness, I ask for divine healing, for You are the Great Physician. I claim the promises of the Holy Bible and speak healing, in Jesus' name. I use my God-given parental authority to stand for my child in faith and to receive divine intervention.

Protect my family. Watch over us. Keep us well and safe. And remind us to always be grateful for Your loving care. Thank You, heavenly Father.

In Jesus' name we pray, amen.

Scriptures for Thought and Meditation

Watch, stand fast in the faith, be brave, be strong.
1 CORINTHIANS 16:13

Then Jesus answered and said to her, "O woman, great is your faith! Let it be to you as you desire." And her daughter was healed that very hour.
MATTHEW 15:28

My Journal

My belief about supernatural healing:

_____
_____
_____
_____
_____
_____
_____
_____
_____
_____
_____
_____
_____

You were sick when:

_____
_____
_____
_____
_____
_____

_____
_____
_____
_____
_____
_____
_____
_____
_____
_____
_____

God healed you when:

_____
_____
_____
_____
_____
_____
_____
_____
_____
_____
_____
_____
_____
_____
_____
_____

Note

1. "Pediatrician: The Healing Power of Honey." http://www.9news.com/rss/story.aspx?storyid=243681 (accessed February 2012).

15

Cooking with Kids

Jennifer's Journal

Micah is now entering his second year. He just loves to taste new foods. Each one is exciting for him. I love the faces he makes when he likes something, but it's even more fun to see his reaction when I give him something he doesn't like. He wrinkles his little nose and sometimes spits it out, and then laughs.

I pray that he will love nutritious foods that are good for him. It's so important to me because I know the benefits of eating healthy. I know Dan will want to give him ice cream and junk food. Once in a while is okay, but I sure don't want to make it a daily habit. In fact, Micah seems to love my healthy homemade ice cream made with only frozen bananas, mangos and almond milk.

At age one, your baby progressed from puréed foods to finely chopped foods. Now that your toddler has entered his second year, he's ready for more. Solid food will make up approximately 50 percent of his nutrition, but that doesn't mean you have to stop nursing. If you and your baby enjoy nursing, you can do what I did and continue to nurse your baby until he or she is ready to wean.

Healthy Food Choices for Toddlers

| 12 to 18 months | Apricots, grapefruit, grape halves, strawberries*, tomatoes, broccoli, cauliflower, melon, mango, kiwi, papaya, pasta (rice pasta is best), wheat cereal*, honey, pancakes, muffins*, bagels, whole milk*, cottage cheese*, whole eggs*, beef, fish* (salmon) |
| 18 to 24 months | Smoothies, shakes, soups, stews, sandwiches, Barbara's Bakery Hole 'n Oats O-shaped cereal |

* Exercise caution when introducing new foods that might cause an allergic reaction. Please see chapter 8, "Allergies."

God created a vast variety of foods to enjoy; so of course, we want our children to receive pleasure from eating. However, picky eaters are not uncommon at this age. Here are some principles that worked well for my family during mealtime. I hope you will find these helpful, as well.

Trust Your Mothering Instincts

Your toddler is changing rapidly at this stage, so don't be surprised if there are days when she has a voracious appetite for solid foods and then, the next day, she only wants to breast-feed or take a bottle. I was so worried about this with Micah until I talked with our pediatrician. Then I learned it is perfectly normal. There's no need to stress out about rules in books. If you know your child is healthy and happy having food one day and just nursing the next, then be at peace. Trust your God-given motherly instincts. Proverbs 1:8-9 says that the teaching of a mother is an ornament of grace to a child's head. Accept that poetic compliment from the Lord.

Encourage by Example

It's not unusual for some little ones to fear trying unfamiliar foods. But remember, he or she is watching and learning from you. So if he sees you enjoying a certain dish, he'll probably want to try it himself. We found this out when Micah and Malia observed Dan and me enjoying sushi. Both of our kids loved sushi by age two—and by age five, Micah could eat a whole truckload. When a baby reaches the age of about one year, they enjoy sitting on their parents' laps and sampling food off of their plates, especially things like mashed sweet potatoes and cooked, soft veggies like carrots or cauliflower. Usually, my kids sat in a highchair at restaurants, but there were times when they needed to be held; so it worked well to let them share my dinner with me.

One trick I used to get Micah to eat his own food was to place his food on my plate, and then he thought it was mine, and he happily gobbled it up. Sometimes you just have to go with what works, and it's best not to worry too much about it. Paul wrote, "Do not be anxious about anything" (Phil. 4:6, *NIV*). That's good advice for us moms, especially at mealtime.

Try Creativity

There may be times when you need to hide or camouflage certain foods so that your child will receive all the nutrition she needs. Foods like mashed sweet potatoes or applesauce work to mask just about everything. Another strategy: When your toddler opens his mouth for his favorite food, you can switch it up and put in the food you want him to try instead. Sometimes it's all in the presentation. I like to have some fun at mealtime, so I get artistic by serving toast trees, apple fries, avocado boats, fruit kabobs, small cheese cubes, papaya canoes, *wana* (pronounced *vana*) veggies, and animal-shaped pancakes with fruit faces. (Directions are below.) You may have other interesting ideas. Creativity comes from God, and I think God blesses moms with an extra dose. Proverbs 8:12 says, "I, wisdom, dwell with prudence, and find out knowledge and discretion." Sometimes a little prudence is called for!

Don't Stress About the Mess

I must admit, I'm a bit of a clean freak . . . or at least I used to be before our children arrived. I really didn't love the mess that came with feeding a two-year-old, so I did everything I could to minimize the mess. I found that if I gave my toddlers too much food, they would use both of their hands and then I would have a huge mess to clean up. Cute for photos, but that was about it. I quickly figured out that if I encouraged neatness and only gave them a few morsels of finger foods on their tray at a time, it kept me sane, and Micah and Malia fed. But whatever happens, don't rant at your kids. God made children washable. And your house is too!

It's Normal to Get Off Schedule

Three meals and two snacks each day is perfect for you and your little ones. Nevertheless, it's quite common for your 12- to 24-month-old to skip a meal. Don't get alarmed; skipping a meal may be difficult for you, but children need time to learn to listen to internal cues for hunger and fullness. Jesus instructed, "Do not worry about tomorrow" (Matt. 6:34). Focus on today and trust God that your little one will be taken care of tomorrow.

Declare a No-battle Zone

Never force-feed your baby or child, as this could create long-term unhealthy eating habits and lead to obesity later in life. Don't turn mealtime into a battle, which is counter-productive. If your son or daughter is not hungry or feels full, never make her clean her plate. Appetites increase when they're going through a growth spurt and appetites wane afterward. During the second year, children gain weight more slowly, and therefore need less food. Our role as moms and dads is to teach our children about the healthy, nutritious foods our heavenly Father has given us for nourishment and to be thankful for them. If we keep that perspective, we'll enjoy meals more.

Portion Size Is the Key

After your rapidly growing little one turns two, he or she can enjoy the same foods the rest of the family eats. The key is simply to control the portion size appropriately.

Daddy's Blog

Okay, I have to be honest here. I am really struggling with this topic, because Jennifer is not the best cook in the world—I mean, she doesn't make the delicious but fattening kinds of food I love to eat. I come from a big Italian family where everyone is a great cook—unhealthy, but tasty—so this has been a big adjustment for me. To her credit, Jen does make some terrific things, like . . . well, salads, shakes, wraps and granola.

Early on, I thought it was important to stress that *everyone* has a job and a role in our mealtime. We started by giving Micah the chore of making sure everyone had something to drink for dinner. Then when Malia was old enough, she was in charge of helping set the table with placemats, silverware and napkins.

When we got married, Jen and I had a deal that if one of us cooked, the other one cleaned. Since she is doing the majority of the cooking, I am usually the one doing the dishes. This is my least favorite chore, but I think it's important to show Micah that men do dishes. The other value I hope we are instilling in our children is that everyone helps. We all eat; therefore, we all need to contribute in some way.

That's a good life lesson that applies to other areas as well.

Your Budding Chef

It's so much fun when your children are old enough to join you in the kitchen. Both Micah and Malia love to help me with everything, from washing the veggies for a stir-fry, to spinning the lettuce for salads. Give your kids jobs that help them learn about measuring, cooking and cleaning. It will give them a lot of satisfaction to help prepare the family meal.

Most days when I'm cooking, I have my children with me in the kitchen to participate. I want them to understand it takes work to prepare a nice meal, and I want them to appreciate the food God has blessed us with. I try to make their jobs simple yet fun. One of the first chores they have is to help put away the dishes, usually the Tupperware and the silverware, no knives or breakables. Next, I let them stand on a stepstool, and I show them how to wash the veggies for dinner. They think that it is absolutely the most fun job in the kitchen. Depending on what I'm making that day, I allow them to use the measuring cups and spoons to assist me with the recipe I'm making.

Directions for Creative, Fun Foods for Kids

Earlier, I wrote about using creativity to make healthy foods for kids. Here's how to make some simple snacks.

Toast Trees

Toast whole grain bread (no white bread, please), then add a favorite topping like a small amount of butter and jelly. (We love the 100 percent fruit-juice-sweetened jelly.) Cut the toast into strips and arrange them into a trunk and branches to create a toast tree.

Apple Fries

Wash and cut an apple to look like little French fry sticks. Serve with almond butter or goat cheese.

Avocado Boats

Cut an avocado in half and remove the seed. Mix your favorite dressing and pour into the boat. My kids love olive oil and balsamic vinegar with a touch of garlic and salt.

Fruit Kabobs

These frozen treats are a favorite summertime snack. Use a kabob stick and alternate pieces of mango, pineapple, strawberries, bananas and peaches. (Just about any fruit will do.) Freeze in a gallon-size Ziploc bag overnight and enjoy the next day.

Papaya Canoes

When we visit my mom in Hawaii, we make these every morning for breakfast. Slice a papaya in half and scoop out the seeds. Dice pineapple, mango and strawberries, and add in blueberries and blackberries if you like. Toss and fill papaya canoe with fruit. Garnish with a mint leaf for the sail.

Wana Veggies

(Hawaiians call the sea urchin a *wana*.) I just made this one up the other day. Scoop 1 to 2 tablespoons of hummus into a small bowl. Cut celery, cucumbers and large carrots into tall, thin sticks. Poke them into the hummus (to look like *wana* spikes) and serve.

Animal-shaped Pancakes with Fruit Faces

Prepare whole wheat or whole grain pancake batter. (We love Pamela's Products: Gluten-Free Baking and Pancake Mix.) Pour a large circle for the face and add smaller circles for the ears. Let your children create the eyes, nose and mouth with sliced bananas, blackberries, blueberries, raspberries or other fruit. Drizzle 100 percent pure maple syrup over the pancake. Enjoy!

Healthy Snack Recipes

In chapter 5, I shared recipes for a smoothie and a pizza. Here are five additional favorite healthy snack recipes my family enjoys.

Mango (or Fruit) Yogurt Parfait (super easy)

⅓ portion of a small yogurt (we love coconut milk yogurt)
Sliced fresh mango (or any kind of fruit)
Toasted walnuts

Layer these in a parfait glass or equivalent. Repeat twice more to create layers.

Peanut Butter "Ice Cream" (one of my favorites)

1 cup almond or rice milk
1–2 large frozen bananas
1 tablespoon peanut butter or almond butter

Blend well, and then freeze. Makes 2–3 servings.

Blue Corn Chips with Chunky Guacamole
(yummy, yet healthy)

2 avocados
1 medium tomato, seeded and diced
¼ cup onion, peeled and diced
⅛ cup cilantro leaves, coarsely chopped
1 tablespoon lime juice
¼ teaspoon cumin
salt and pepper to taste

Mash the avocados with the back of a fork or other utensil. Add the cumin, onion and cilantro. Stir in lime juice. Add salt and pepper to taste. Fold the avocado and tomato together. *Serve immediately. Make sure you let the kids help you with this.*

Homemade Potato Wedges (Dan's favorite)

1 pound baby red potatoes, cut into wedges
½ cup olive oil
½ cup Parmesan cheese
1 tablespoon Mrs. Dash® seasoning (MSG-free)
salt and pepper to taste

Pour olive oil, cheese, and seasoning over potato wedges. Bake 45 minutes at 350° F.

Sweet Potato Fries (Micah's and Malia's favorite)

2 large sweet potatoes
2 to 3 tablespoons olive oil
salt and pepper to taste

Wash and cut sweet potatoes into strips and place into a large Ziploc bag. Pour in just enough oil to coat the potatoes, and then add salt and pepper to taste. Close bag and toss until coated. Arrange fries on a cookie sheet. Bake at 350° F for 25–35 minutes.

Deuteronomy 8:8 records that God gave His people "a land of wheat and barley, of vines and fig trees and pomegranates, a land of olive oil and honey." This is a picture showing God's goodness and provision. We are always aware of God's goodness and grateful to Him when we enjoy a meal; and we teach our children to do the same.

Parent's Prayer

Dear Heavenly Father,

Thank You so very much for blessing us with food to eat. We pray for the people throughout this world who have nothing or too little to eat. Open our eyes to what we can do to help. We want to be people who give from our abundance. We commit to give to others, both near and far, who are lacking food—especially children. Let us never take for granted what we have. Give us generous hearts to share with others.

Jesus, please help me to make wise choices for my family's meals. Help me teach my children what is healthy and nutritious to take care of their bodies as the temple of the Holy Spirit.

And help me to remember to enjoy this time in my life. There are days when cooking is such a chore, and I don't want to do it; give me an attitude that pleases You, Lord.

Thank You, Jesus, for Your many blessings, both physical and spiritual. We pray this in Your holy name, amen.

Scriptures for Thought and Meditation

And God said, "See, I have given you every herb that yields s eed which is on the face of all the earth, and every tree whose fruit yields seed; to you it shall be for food."
GENESIS 1:29

And when he had said these things, he took bread, and gave thanks to God in the presence of them all; and when he had broken it he began to eat.
ACTS 27:35

My Journal

Some of my favorite jobs in the kitchen were:

_____
_____
_____
_____
_____
_____
_____
_____
_____
_____
_____
_____
_____

Some of our favorite family recipes:

_____
_____
_____
_____
_____
_____
_____
_____
_____
_____
_____
_____
_____
_____
_____
_____
_____
_____
_____

16

Education Starts at Home

Jennifer's Journal

Micah loves to learn. He is memorizing Bible verses, shapes, colors, numbers, the names of many different animals, the planets in our solar system, the Hawaiian islands, and the names of the 44 presidents of the United States. He also counts to 10 in 10 different languages. We work on learning every day while he's eating breakfast or lunch, and I try to make a game of it and draw everything out on large poster board so he can see it visually as well as hear it spoken.

It's amazing to see his two-year-old mind work. Thank You, Lord, for giving my child the joy of learning. Help me to teach him what is important and necessary to thrive in this world today, and help me to teach him about You, Jesus.

You are your baby's first teacher. I think that is pretty special. Later on, you might delegate some of the responsibility to daycare providers, teachers and, eventually, to college professors; but first and foremost, it is up to you to make sure your child receives good teaching. Truly, education starts at home.

I take this to heart and spend many hours teaching my kids, every opportunity I get. No matter where we go, I try to make their world a classroom. For example, when we visit my parents in Hawaii, I love to take them to the beach and walk with them in the tide pools. I show them different creatures that God made, like *wana* (sea urchins); *a'ama* crabs (black crabs that are a local favorite); *opihi* shells (small clams that stick themselves to the rock); *loli* (sea cucumbers); *limu* (edible seaweed); and of course, the Hawaiian green sea turtles. We absolutely love to make every day an adventure, no matter where we are.

At the farmers market in Hawaii, my children love to learn about the local foods, like *lilikoi* (passion fruit), star fruit, guava or *mochi* ice cream, which is a Japanese delight. It's such fun to see their expressions when they get to taste these special treats.

All kinds of everyday tasks can be educational. Going shopping is an opportunity to teach children about money. Even when they're young, they can learn that the family has a budget and there is a difference between necessities and luxuries, and that giving to God is part of the budget.

Gardening is another way to teach children about planting, sowing and reaping. They learn that when they work, they will reap the benefits from their labor.

Of course, education takes place inside and outside the home. Here are some considerations when looking at the alternatives.

Choosing a Good Daycare

Many moms are in a position where finding a daycare provider is a top priority. There are many daycare providers who do a wonderful job; so if you're in a position where going back to work is a requirement, you won't have to worry about your child or feel bad about your time away from him or her. Options include (1) professional childcare centers, (2) licensed family daycare often provided by another mom in her home, (3) in-home care in which a nanny or babysitter comes to your house, and (4) care given by relatives or friends.

Word of mouth is your best bet when it comes to making a good choice. You can ask friends and parents in your church for recommendations. If another parent can't say enough good things about a certain daycare, stop in to visit the facility, both to observe and to talk with the teachers. An unscheduled visit will enable you to get a more accurate picture of a typical day.

Have a list of questions ready so you can determine if the facility's childcare philosophy matches your own. You'll want to ask about how they handle behavior issues, what the teacher-to-child ratio is, whether or not they have an educational program, as well as what their policy is for sick days and late pick-up (in cases where you might be required to work late). You also want to see the kitchen and bathroom and look for cleanliness. Ask about accident reports. Make sure there is adequate space for the number of children and that the toys are age-appropriate. In some states, licensing is required.

Two helpful websites that link parents with childcare professionals are www.Bradadoo.com and www.AngiesList.com. Child-Care Aware is a service that links childcare providers and families. They have a hotline (1-800-424-2246) and a website, www.child careaware.org.

After you've chosen your childcare provider, do drop in for a surprise visit from time to time to build your confidence in the provider and give you peace of mind.

In addition to praying for God's guidance in choosing the right caregiver for your precious child, pray for the childcare providers and for God to bless them with the fruit of the Spirit: love, joy, peace, patience, kindness, goodness, faithfulness, gentleness and self-control (see Gal. 5:22-23). I don't know of a teacher, nanny, mother or grandparent who wouldn't love to know someone is praying for her workday to go well.

Formal Education

When it comes time to choose formal education for your son or daughter, I encourage you, once again, to make it a matter of prayer. As you do your research, ask God to lead and guide you to the right choice for your child, and I believe the Holy Spirit will speak to your heart and give you peace about the decision you make.

We are blessed to live in a country where we have choices for our children's education. The right choice is not "one size fits all." One child may flourish in a home environment where the mom is a savvy one-on-one teacher; another child might need a classroom to bring about his or her best development. Here is some input that I hope will help you make good decisions for your own child.

Nana's Journal

When my children were young, I made an appointment to visit two classrooms at a local Christian school. I was allowed to sit in the back and observe for 30 minutes.

The first class was amazing. The class president opened with the Pledge of Allegiance and then handed the floor to the class secretary who proceeded to read the "minutes": a summary of the lessons from the day before, including a reminder to study for the upcoming spelling test. She then turned the class over to the teacher who held the class in rapt attention with her interesting lesson.

My second class visit was a startling contrast. The teacher read in a monotone with his nose in a book while the kids threw spit wads and even a book across the classroom.

I observed the best and the worst classes I'd ever seen in the same school.

Carolyn Warren

Public School

I did not have a good experience in the public school system during my middle and high school years, so I was very much against sending my own children to public school. National testing showed the school I attended was behind in academics; and drinking, drugs and sex were the norm in the higher-grade levels. When my parents finally put me into a private Christian school, in the sixth grade, it was too late. I hated the new school and wanted to go back to my friends. I got kicked out of school in the seventh grade, and my parents were forced to send me back to the public school the next year. I wish I hadn't been so rebellious, but I was carrying so much hurt inside (please see my testimony in chapter 23).

I also believe that a child *can* succeed no matter how bad the public school is. I attended Konaweana, the same school Hawaii's first astronaut graduated from just years before I did. Onizuka was an achiever by choice. He didn't get caught up in the drinking and drugs like so many others did, including myself.

Where we live now, the public schools are *much better*. It all depends on your location and who the teacher is. I strongly recommend meeting the teacher who will be assigned to your child. Most schools will allow parents to observe the classroom with a prior appointment; and even though the teacher will know you're coming, this visit can be very revealing.

You'll want to be aware of the curriculum so you can teach your children at home what you believe to be biblical truth in contrast to unproven hypotheses or anti-Christian philosophies that might be presented at school. For example, what does the school teach about the origin of the earth, creation versus evolution, family values, sex education, Eastern religions?

Laying a firm foundation and teaching children about Jesus during these early years is ever so important. I highly recommend you make it a priority to be involved in the classroom as much as possible if you do enroll your child in public school.

Private Christian School

This was my first choice for our children even before they were born, because I felt that my younger siblings who grew up in a Christian school had such an advantage. They have followed the Lord throughout their lives and went on to do mission trips; and a couple of them became missionaries. They never got involved in drinking or fell away from God, like I did during my teens and twenties. I believe it was mostly due to the difference in their school influences, especially during those critical teenage years.

The cost of private school is the most common reason why more parents don't send their children to a Christian school. I completely understand that. There were many months when we didn't know if we could keep Micah enrolled in his school. We sold my car, stopped all eating out, did absolutely no shopping except for food and necessities, cut back everywhere we possibly could and started selling items on Craig's List. Dan was working three jobs at the time, and I was just about to take on a waitressing job to help pay for Micah's schooling when God finally answered our prayers. So I do understand and know firsthand what it's like to barely make ends meet and to sacrifice for your child's Christian schooling.

Many schools offer financial aid, even if they don't advertise it, and I encourage you to explore that option if you need help. Taking on a second or third job may be another choice for you as well. I believe the financial sacrifice is worth the benefit for your child's future.

Homeschool

Now that Malia is three and Micah has turned six, Dan and I have just agreed to homeschool our children during these younger years. We will supplement it with a one- to two-day a week school to make sure that we are giving our children a proper education and a chance to make friends and interact with their peers.

I believe that there are many benefits to homeschooling. I am looking forward to instilling good morals and values throughout my children's day, giving them a well-rounded education and building a strong family unit. I believe this will also give them a chance to excel in their academics, as homeschoolers' test scores are typically above average. It will allow them to be more creative and to truly use their imagination, both in and outside of the classroom. It is also healthier, because I will be able to give them nutritious snacks and lunches without having to worry about them trading meals with someone. Another plus will be that my kids won't have to stay indoors all day.

We can take a nature walk for their science class, and PE is always outside, weather permitting. (In 2006, the National Parent Teacher Association reported that nearly 40 percent of American elementary schools have eliminated or are considering eliminating recess.[1]) I believe they already get plenty of social interaction through Sunday School, Awana, MOPS, swim class, gymnastics, sports, traveling— you name it. They are not deprived socially.

In Dr. James Dobson's book *Bringing Up Boys*, he says that if given the chance to do it over again, he and his wife, Shirley, would probably have homeschooled their children. He goes on to explain that kids who are homeschooled are not isolated but have support groups, field trips, tutoring available and teaching co-ops. There are also numerous outings to go on such as visiting museums, parks, trips to farms, factories, hospitals, seats with the local government, days with dad to the office, trips to Grandma's, extracurricular activities such as music and sports, and so much more. I recommend that you pray and consider this option if you feel it is right for your family.

I know that this decision is not for everyone. If you decide to homeschool your children, there is an abundance of information available on blogs, websites and in books to help you. I recommend asking around at your local churches to find a homeschooling group that can help you with any questions you may have, as well as doing adequate research.

An amazing mom who inspired me to homeschool was Michelle Dugger. Last year we met at her hotel when her whole family was in Colorado to do a book signing at the Focus on the Family station. We sat and talked for more than an hour and a half. What a wonderful Christian woman who loves the Lord—and she is a mother of 19! That's right, 19 children, and she has homeschooled every one of them. She told me how wonderful it was to be with her children throughout the day and to teach them the values and character qualities that were important to her family. She went on to explain that she and her husband, Jim Bob, want to train their children to become mature Christians who love God and to shape them into responsible leaders. I hope to do the same with my children.

While some of us prefer the homeschool approach, others, such as my co-author Carolyn Warren, prefer private Christian school. However, for financial reasons, parents may be unable to provide this form of education. If you have concerns about not being adequately equipped to provide quality education at home, especially in subjects such as higher math and science, there are tutors and supplemental schools that are just one or two days per week that partner with the homeschooling parents. This way your child can have a variety—and even the challenges—that come with having a classroom of peers.

No matter what type of schooling you choose, that first day will be a very special day. I vividly remember that first day of preschool for Micah. He had a large cut on his chin from falling the week before. I made special homemade pancakes and fresh fruit for breakfast, and we packed his snack in his little backpack. We dropped him off for preschool, Dan and I acting as happy as we could. We held hands as we left the tall, brick building, leaving our firstborn behind.

As soon as we got into the parking lot, we both broke down. Tears streamed down my face as I cried, "Why does he have to go to school? He's not ready!" In reality, I didn't want to let go of my son. I wanted to homeschool him, but at that time Dan did not agree with me on this matter. I am so thankful that through three years of praying, God has answered my heart's desire to be able to teach my children at home while they are young.

During the years that Micah did attend preschool and kindergarten outside of our home, I did my best to help him enjoy going to school. He looked forward to the notes that I hid in his shoes from time to time and the yummy snacks I'd pack in his bag each day. He loved the times that I volunteered to read during parent story time and the times I was the parent helper in his class.

There are academic choices to consider, but no matter where your children go to receive their education, keep your children in daily prayer. The apostle wrote these encouraging words, which make a good prayer to personalize about your child: "Be assured that from the first day we heard of you, we haven't stopped praying for you, asking God to give you wise minds and spirits attuned to his will, and so acquire a thorough understanding of the ways in which God works. We pray that you'll live well for the Master, making him proud of you" (Col. 1:9-10, *THE MESSAGE*).

If you don't have a prayer partner, I encourage you to connect with other women in prayer by joining Moms in Prayer, International. This organization has groups—including mothers, grandmas, aunties and other women—who gather together to pray for their children and schools, from preschool through college. Please visit www.MomsInTouch.org for more information.

Parent's Prayer

Dear Jesus,

You lived a life of learning from God, Your Father, and then You taught Your disciples and the multitudes of people. Help me also to learn from God, my heavenly Father. Give me spiritual ears to hear what He is saying to me, both through my church leaders and through the Holy Spirit in my heart. Give me a greater understanding of the Bible as I read it. Enlighten my mind and heart so that Your Word becomes alive and relevant. Speak to me through the Scriptures and let me learn from You.

Help me to be the best teacher and mentor for my child that I can possibly be. Help me to effectively pass on my knowledge and understanding. Give me ideas for explaining lessons and principles so that he/she will understand. Give me patience in teaching so that my tone of voice is not sharp or intimidating. Give me wisdom to pass on to my child.

I desire a Holy Spirit anointing to teach the Scriptures to my child. I want to pass on a love of Your Word. Let me pass on a love of language, of reading, of mathematics, of science. Give me discernment to know what natural talents and abilities my child has so that I can encourage him/her in that direction.

And, Lord Jesus, direct me in choosing the right education or school for my child. Your Word promises that if I acknowledge You in all things, You will direct my paths; so I stand on that promise and ask You to direct me in choosing the right educational path for my dear son/daughter. In Jesus' name I pray, amen.

Scriptures for Thought and Meditation

Wisdom begins with fear and respect for the L ORD. Knowledge of the Holy One leads to understanding.
PROVERBS 9:10, ERV

My son, hear the instruction of your father, and do not forsake the law of your mother; for they will be a graceful ornament on your head, and chains about your neck.
PROVERBS 1:8-9

My Journal

A memorable educational moment at home:

_____

_____

_____

_____

_____

I chose this form of schooling for you _____
_____because . . .

At a young age, you showed signs of being good at . . .

Note
1. Rose Garrett, "Why Kids Learn Less When Schools Get Rid of Recess," January 19, 2010. http://news.change.org/stories/why-kids-learn-less-when-schools-get-rid-of-recess (accessed July 2012).

17

There's a New Baby
in the Family

Jennifer's Journal

Last week, Micah and I were in the living room when he looked at me and said very matter-of-factly, "Mommy, you have a baby in your tummy."

Shocked, I said, "Oh, no, honey, we just started trying," knowing he didn't know what "trying" meant, as he was only 22 months old.

"No, mommy, you have a baby in your tummy!" he said. I just smiled and continued folding the laundry.

Now wouldn't you know it, two weeks later I took a pregnancy test, and Micah was right! I checked the calendar and there was only one time that we could have conceived two-and-a half weeks earlier. It had been the following morning that my son told me I was pregnant.

I believe God does amazing things and can definitely speak through our children.

Those words Micah spoke to me sat in the back of my head for more than two weeks until I finally decided to see if I really was pregnant. I got the pregnancy test out, peed on the stick and put it the bathroom sink. I went and got the video camera and then called Dan in from the living room to check the results. I filmed him as he walked out of the bathroom holding the stick, and with a tear in his eye exclaimed, "We're pregnant . . . again!"

In that moment, our whole family got excited, but Micah was especially happy. He jumped and danced around the house for what seemed like an hour.

During the next few months, a day didn't go by that Micah didn't kiss my tummy and pray for his baby sister. We never found out officially that it was a girl, but I just knew it. As Micah watched my tummy grow, he'd talk to our baby and tell her all the fun they were going to have with his racecars and Thomas the Tank Engine train set.

Time seemed to fly by during this pregnancy with Malia, and it was completely different from my pregnancy with Micah. I was healthy and active, but I was in excruciating pain during my fifth month. When the week before Thanksgiving arrived, I couldn't even walk. I got sciatica so bad that I couldn't even pick up my little boy anymore, let alone nurse him at night. I couldn't lay down in bed with him to say his prayers with him, so instead I'd just hang over the side, kind of kneeling next to his toddler bed. I had never known such pain! Even the 30-plus hours of natural childbirth with Micah did not compare to this. And nothing I tried seemed to take away the pain—not the swimming, stretching or walking.

Finally, I couldn't take it anymore. I got down on my knees and literally cried out to God.

The next day I went to a prenatal chiropractor without results. A few days after that I went to see my regular chiropractor, Dr. Pesta, and he tried to help me as well. I walked into his office and broke down in tears. He gave me an adjustment and tried to help the baby move off of the nerve; but again, nothing seemed to help. He shared an office with Dr. Stebbins, my acupuncturist who had helped me with my allergies in the past. He offered to try, and I jumped at the chance. He gently placed a few tiny needles in strategic places, and wouldn't you know it—those little needles took away most of the pain. I could finally function again. Praise God!

A few months later, Malia was born. (Her birth story is in our first book, *Praying Through Your Pregnancy*.) Her labor and delivery were much shorter than Micah's, and we were extremely grateful for God's grace during that time. In fact, her middle name is Grace, just for that reason. And from the minute she arrived, Micah was thrilled to have a little sister. He had been a meaningful part of the pregnancy as I had included him on every doctor visit. At each appointment, he held the monitor for the doctor and we'd listen to Malia's heartbeat together and guess if our baby was going to be a girl or a boy. So when March 19 arrived, and Micah finally got to see his sister, he held her little hand and kissed her head and said, "Hi, Baby, I'm your big brother. I will always be here for you, and I will protect you." It was so sweet it brought tears to my eyes.

I wanted to preserve those good feelings that Micah had toward his new sister. So when we got home, I took steps to keep him from feeling left out or overshadowed by Malia. I wrapped up a special gift and made sure that Micah knew it was from his sister. When we got home from the hospital, Cranky the Crane was waiting for him, *from Malia*. I wanted him to know that the baby was very happy to have him as a big brother. I also knew that since new babies sleep a lot, I could use that time to give Micah my attention and get some cleaning done. For example, when Malia was napping, I organized Micah's books and then read him a couple stories, or I organized his games and then played one with him.

To make Micah feel like he was a "Big Helper," I asked him to get me Malia's diapers and her little clothes when I needed them. I even let him help me carefully bathe and dress her.

Then at night, when Dan got home, Dan spent special Daddy/Micah time, just playing with him and doing boy stuff like racecars or trains. When they were finished, I'd give Malia to Dan while I took Micah upstairs for his bath and bed, which gave me a little more one-on-one time with my son.

Another idea to help your older child is to give him or her a doll or "baby animal" to take care of. I had a sling for Malia to ride in all day, and Micah really wanted one, too, for his lion or Malia's baby doll that she had just received. I sewed him a little sling, and he walked around the house with "*his* baby" in it.

At times, when Malia cried, I had Micah go over and sing to her or rock her in her swing. This made him feel needed as well.

On Malia's first birthday, I took Micah out to choose a gift for her from him, and I made sure she also had a gift to give him—a new soccer ball.

Potty Training

Another way to make Micah feel like the Big Boy in the House was to get him potty trained. Besides, I didn't want two babies in diapers at the same time, and he was ready at last. I had made mistakes in the past and tried to push him into potty training when he was too young. But now he was over two years old, and he was ready. I found that these tips worked well for us.

1. Never force your baby to potty train too early. I had someone tell me that all of her four children were trained by 14 months old, so I felt pressured to teach Micah at 18 months—*and it didn't work.* Children are ready at different ages.

2. Teach your toddler by example. If you have a boy, daddy will do a better job at showing your son how to stand and pee-pee than mommy can. The dilemma

here is that moms are usually the ones who are home; but the plus here is that girls usually learn at an earlier age, because they have mom to show them how.

3. Can your child take her pants off by herself? Toilet training is a complex skill, and multiple tasks must be performed in the correct sequence. In addition to pulling down her own pants, does she feel the urge and can she get there in time, and can she sit down on the toilet before it's too late? Be as patient as possible.

4. Get a cool potty seat—we got a sports-theme seat for Micah, and he absolutely loved it. He wanted to sit on it even when he didn't have to go potty.

5. Use stickers or a reward chart. This worked great for both of my kids. I made a cute chart, and if they earned enough stickers in one day, they won a special treat.

6. Don't use Pull-Ups or diapers at night—at least, not for very long. I made that mistake too. I was so tired of changing yet another wet bed and washing another load of sheets, that I kept diapers or Pull-Ups on Micah until he was older. But instead of helping, it actually hurt his ability in learning how to get up at night to use the potty. If you're tired of wet sheets, you can get super-large hospital pads to put under your little one. Then just toss them when they get wet so you won't have to wash the bedding again.

Even though you do all these things, your child may still have accidents from time to time. Accidents are just that—accidents. Therefore, it's key not to get mad or yell at your child.

I'll never forget the morning when my little guy woke me up. "Mom, I had an accident down on the tile in the kitchen."

"It's okay; Mommy will clean it," I said half asleep. I rolled out of bed and proceeded to walk down the stairs, and sure enough, he had a *big* accident, but the kicker was that he had accidently stepped in it and there was a trail of poop all the way upstairs on every other carpeted step. After I cried, I laughed it off and cleaned it up.

Siblings: As Best Friends

Micah was, and still is, such a good helper with his little sis. From the first day they met, they have been best friends. For more than four years now, they have been inseparable. They do everything together and truly love being together. I can honestly say that the majority of the time, they get along just fine. Do they ever squabble or fight? Of course they do; but not very often. I believe that God answered my prayers. While I was pregnant with Malia, I prayed daily that my children would become best friends and get along wonderfully—and I encourage you to do the same. Prayer is a powerful and effective gift you can give your children, and it keeps your home much more peaceful.

We know from reading Matthew 13:55-56 and Mark 3:31 that Jesus grew up with brothers and sisters. And we know from Hebrews 4:15 that Jesus was "in all points tempted as we are." So this tells us Jesus understands sibling rivalry and the temptations that go along with it. And yet, Jesus was without sin. Jesus did not get into selfish fights with His siblings. Can you imagine what it would have been like to have Jesus as your older brother? One thing I'm sure of is that Jesus was loving and handled His relationships just right.

I think the Scriptures show that Jesus and His siblings were a close family. Jesus' brothers and His mother, Mary, traveled together with Jesus down to Capernaum for the wedding where Jesus performed the first miracle of turning the water into wine (see John 2:12). The Bible doesn't give us much information about Jesus' sisters, but Jesus' brother James became the leader of the church in Jerusalem (see Acts 12:17; 15:13), and Jesus' brother Jude is probably the one who wrote the book of Jude in the New Testament. Incidentally, we know that all of Jesus' brothers were married, according to 1 Corinthians 9:5.

But even more relevant to us today is that Jesus regarded all of God's children as *His own family*. Mark 3:34-35 tells us that Jesus looked at the circle of people around Him and said, "Here are My mother and My brothers! For whoever does the will of God is My brother and My sister and mother." Now that's something to think about! Jesus regards you and me as His own sister or brother.

Parent's Prayer

Dear Jesus,

Thank You for accepting me into Your family. When I think about how awesome it is to be a part of Your family for eternity, I feel humbled, grateful and very glad. Help me to remember that, during times of trial and temptation, so that I choose to respond to others as You would. Help me to follow Your example, always honoring others and showing kindness.

And, Lord, I thank You for the new baby I have on the way. When he or she is born, give us a smooth transition. Guide me in making sure my older child does not feel left out or overshadowed by the new baby. Show me how to spend quality one-on-one time with him/her. I pray against sibling jealousy and rivalry. I pray for a spirit of peace over our home. I pray that my children will get along with one another, that they will become close and dear friends for a lifetime.

Lord Jesus, as the time gets closer for our family to grow, help me to grow in Your love. Let me draw closer to You every day. I pray that the words of Scripture would light up in my soul. Speak to me through Your Holy Word. Show me the path, and direct my steps.

In Jesus' wonderful name I pray, amen.

Scriptures for Thought and Meditation

Finally, brothers and sisters, rejoice! Strive for full restoration, encourage one another, be of one mind, live in peace. And the God of love and peace will be with you.
2 CORINTHIANS 13:11, TNIV

Be kindly affectionate to one another with brotherly love,
in honor giving preference to one another.
ROMANS 12:10

My Journal

When your brother/sister was born, you were _____ years old.
Your reaction was . . .

_____

_____

_____

_____

_____

_____

_____

_____

_____

_____

_____

_____

I helped you feel special by . . .

_____

_____

_____

_____

_____

_____

_____

_____

_____

_____

_____

_____

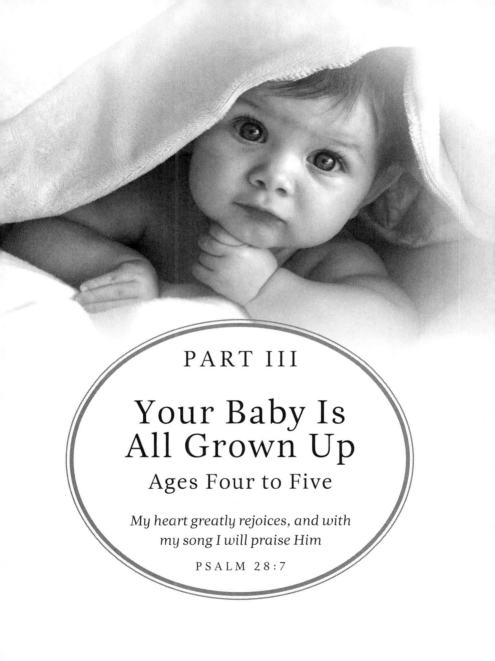

PART III

Your Baby Is All Grown Up

Ages Four to Five

My heart greatly rejoices, and with my song I will praise Him

PSALM 28:7

18

Mommy's Little Helper

Jennifer's Journal

Micah is at the age when he wants to help me with everything. It is so nice having an enthusiastic little worker. He loves to help put away the dishes and silverware (after I do the knives, of course). He also enjoys helping me cook, clean and fold the laundry. He's especially helpful when it comes to Malia. He likes to dunk her diapers in the basket and run upstairs and get me a clean little outfit for her whenever she needs a change.

What a blessing to have a helper! There are days when I feel so overwhelmed with all the housework I just don't know what to do. And now I just signed a contract to write a prayer book on pregnancy ... my husband thinks I'm crazy. Micah is two-and-a-half years old, and Malia just turned three months old. Lord, please help me to be a great mother and a good wife, and to write the words that You want me to share with other women.

Malia was only four months old when I starting writing *Praying Through Your Pregnancy* along with my Godsend co-author, Carolyn Warren. I didn't know how I was going to do it all, but I clearly felt God speaking to me to write that book. I decided that the best time to write was late at night when everyone was sleeping, but that was usually when I'd clean the house. So our home was not in tip-top shape that summer. Fortunately, I soon learned that I was not the only one who could clean up the house.

I'd always taught Micah to be my helper. So at a very early age he began to take care of certain "mini jobs." I believe that children are much more capable of some responsibility than we sometimes think they are. They just need to be taught and guided as they learn new things. I quickly realized that when Micah got to help out around the house, his self-confidence grew as he felt like he was contributing to our family. God designed families to work together and for each member to feel valuable.

Many toddlers are very eager to help mommy around the house. If you're not quite sure what kind of jobs are appropriate, here is a handy list that worked for us. Remember to always be appreciative of their willingness to help—regardless of how proficient they are—and to keep their excitement alive so they will continue to have this good attitude toward service in the future.

How Two- and Three-Year-Olds Can Help
- Help make the bed and change the sheets
- Pick up their toys and books
- Take laundry to the laundry room
- Help put clean clothes away; put away shoes
- Fold washcloths
- Toss dirty laundry in the hamper
- Help wipe up messes
- Mop, with help (we like the Swiffer)
- Dust the furniture
- Set out napkins on the dining table
- Help feed the pets

How Four- and Five-Year-Olds Can Help
Your child can assist you with these chores at first then slowly progress to doing them independently.

- Set the table or help set the table
- Put away toys and their belongings

- Water the plants around the house
- Help make the beds
- Dust higher up around the house
- Sort clothes by color for the laundry
- Help load the dishwasher
- Water the garden, rake leaves, help with planting, shovel dirt using child-size garden tools
- Help wipe up messes
- Help clear the table after meals
- Vacuum, with a small-sized vacuum
- Help put away groceries
- Feed and water the pets

Nana's Journal

When my grandchildren come to visit, they love to help me out.

In the summer, I'll set up one child with the garden hose and give the other a watering can. They have so much fun watering the flowers and ferns. It keeps them busy for the longest time.

In the autumn, I give them each a large bag and we set out to gather pinecones.

In winter, there's always something they can help me with indoors. Last week, my granddaughters had a ball helping me reorganize my rubber stamp collection. They were quite adept at separating the stamps into categories.

For me, it's all about bonding. Maintaining a close relationship with my granddaughters and grandson is a priority for me. For this reason, I will always need their help. As they mature, the projects will change, but we'll always have fun together.

Carolyn Warren

Whenever possible, I like to make chores seem like a game. When my children hit the kindergarten age, they were still excited about helping out and usually thrilled when I took the time to teach them how to do a new task. I found that rewards at this age were fun and motivating, so I created chore charts and award stickers for small chores, and then I let them work up to bigger rewards for more labor-intensive jobs. For example, if my kids earn 20 stickers, we go to the dollar store or a garage sale and they get to pick out a toy or coloring book. Many times the chores have been completed only by my help every step of the way, and that's okay. At this point, you are laying the groundwork for your children to learn that working and helping out are a part of life.

If you're not into designing charts yourself, you can download free charts for almost any behavior you want to encourage at http://www.freeprintablebehaviorcharts.com/chore_list.htm.

For example, there's a chart for household chores, bedtime routine, feeding the dog or cat, brushing teeth, having a good attitude, and many more. I've used some of them myself, and my kids absolutely love charting their progress. For some preschoolers, connecting chores to an allowance (or commission, as we call it) is a great option. It fosters independence and enables them to begin to learn about money and saving for something they want to purchase.

Malia seems to be growing up so fast. She wanted to help with everything at a very young age. I think it was because she saw her older brother doing various tasks, so she automatically thought she could do them as well. At three years old now, she is a tremendous help, and she loves to vacuum, and to squirt and wash the windows.

The Ministry of Helping

Are you one of those people who love to help out in your church? Do you volunteer to bring a hot dish, help keep the church clean or watch the babies in the nursery? The gift of helps is listed as one of the vital ministries of the Christian church. That's right! You'll find it named right along with apostles, prophets, teachers, miracles, and the gifts of healing (see 1 Cor. 12:28).

This is an area in which I pray my children will learn from the deeds I do. We are to serve others, and if they see me deliver a meal to a mom with a new baby, watch a child because a friend is sick, or help a homeless person, they will learn to serve others as well.

Parent's Prayer

Dear Heavenly Father,

Thank You for my little one who is growing up and becoming a helper. Please help me show patience when he/she is trying to help and I know I could do it faster alone. Remind me that it's not about getting the task done; it's about raising my child to have good character. I want to be both a good mentor and a good example.

Lord, show me if there is a way I should be helping more in my church. Even though I'm a busy parent, I never want to be too busy for You. Give me a heart to volunteer for areas in which I'm capable. Bless my abilities and talents to be used for Your kingdom.

Thank You for all You have blessed me with. I thank You that I have a home to clean and clothes that need laundering. I thank You that we have groceries to put away and meals to clean up after. Let me see the chores I have to do with eyes of gratitude for all You have blessed me with. In Jesus' name, amen.

Scriptures for Thought and Meditation

As each one has received a gift, minister it to one another, as good stewards of the manifold grace of God.
1 PETER 4:10

Then the King will say to those on His right hand, "Come, you blessed of My Father, inherit the kingdom prepared for you from the foundation of the world: for I was hungry and You gave Me food; I was thirsty and you gave Me drink; I was a stranger and you took Me in; I was naked and you clothed Me; I was sick and you visited Me; I was in prison and you came to Me."
MATTHEW 25:34–36

My Journal

When you were two to three years old, your favorite job to help me with was . . .

_____
_____
_____
_____
_____
_____
_____
_____
_____
_____

When you were four to five years old, your favorite job to help me with was . . .

_____
_____
_____
_____
_____
_____
_____
_____
_____
_____
_____

19

Exercise and Sports
for Your Child

Jennifer's Journal

When I met Dan, he was a sportscaster here in Denver. He could tell you just about every player on every team and answer just about any question you'd throw out on the subject. Now, Micah absolutely loves sports, just like his daddy; he's getting into basketball and soccer. We signed him up to play peewee soccer this week, and during the first game he made a goal—for the other team! I laughed so hard; it was so innocent, but Dan wasn't so happy. Oh well, Micah had fun!

I am thankful that my son loves to play sports and keep active. It is such a big part of our family. Whether we are biking around the lake in Estes Park for my birthday; sledding when we get a big bout of snow here in Denver; or kayaking, swimming or boogie boarding in Hawaii, we always try to plan our days around an activity where we get a reasonable amount of exercise.

I believe it is so important to teach our little ones while they are young to enjoy sports and exercise.

As all parents know, kids love to play. But how do you know when your child is ready to join an organized sports team? To determine what's best for your child, you'll want to consider several issues.

Three Considerations Before Joining a Team

1. Are You Looking at an Individual Sport or a Team Sport?

The American Academy of Pediatrics suggests team sports, such as baseball and soccer, beginning at age six and up. For preschool-age children, individual sports, such as gymnastics, swimming or karate, might be more beneficial.[1] The average preschooler has not yet developed the ability to throw or catch a ball, and even following the rules of a game can be a stumbling block. Even with individual sports, there should be a low enough coach-to-participant ratio so that your child doesn't spend too much time standing around waiting.

Some personalities do better at team sports and some at individual sports. One little girl's parents signed her up for a soccer team, but at the games, they noticed she spent all her time sprinting from one end of the field to the other but never got close enough to kick the ball. When they asked her why she didn't ever go in for the ball, she said, "I'm afraid someone will kick me." After that, they signed her up for a dance class, and she absolutely loved it.

Malia knows what she wants to do already. Last week she asked to take a ballet class and gymnastics. We told her when she turned four she could pick the one sport she would like to try first. I want to give my children choices and let them have a say in what they'd like to do. It teaches them they are able to make choices, both good and bad. And if they don't like what they picked, they will at least have to finish the class or semester, because their teammates will be counting on them, and it's not right to just quit something.

2. Has Your Child Developed Sufficient Emotional Maturity?

When you play games at home, how does your child handle losing? If he or she is still having a major meltdown, more "practice games" at home is a good idea. Also, does your child know how to exercise patience and take turns? Can he share with others? Can she hold her attention on a coach and follow directions?

Participating in sports is a wonderful way to further develop these abilities, but you don't want to throw your child into a situation that he or she isn't able to handle. After all, sports are supposed to be fun, not distressing.

3. Has Your Child Expressed an Interest in Playing on a Team or in a Specific Sport?

Forget what your friends' kids are doing. Forget what your nieces and nephews are doing. You're not competing with other parents here. It's perfectly fine if your child is not interested in joining a team. There are many years ahead for that. On the other hand, if your son or daughter has been asking to play soccer or sign up for gymnastics, that's a sign he or she might be ready for the challenge.

When Malia was just past three, we went to the pool and she became terrified of the water. She'd cling to me with a viselike grip, telling me not to let her go. It seemed so odd because the year before she had loved the water. One day, we were on the way to the pool again, and we stopped at a garage sale. The lady had a little pink mask for sale for $1. We scooped it up and headed to the pool. That was the end of her fear. We put the mask on her face and she took her little mermaid doll into the pool with her. I encouraged her to watch her mermaid swim through the water while I held her tight. Before I knew it, she was pushing me away and swimming in the shallow part of the pool on her own.

The next week, I signed up both kids for swim lessons. They went once a week for four months. By the time we traveled to Hawaii in December, Malia could swim all by herself. People would stop me at the beach or pool in Hawaii and ask me how old she was and how I got her to love the water so much. I'd laugh and tell them the story about the mask and the mermaid, and how just a few months earlier she was panicked in the water. Swimming is a "sport" that I think is absolutely vital to teach your children. Kicking a soccer ball is fun, but knowing how to swim can save their lives.

Daddy's Blog

SPORTS—a topic that is near and dear to my heart. I happen to know a little bit about the topic after being a sportscaster for 10 years. (You do realize that sportscasters are frustrated athletes who were never big enough or good enough to be a pro, so we decided to report on the pros.) I am also fiercely competitive at everything, and I mean everything. This is where I have had the most struggles as a dad.

While I can teach the sports and play the sports, I sometimes need to check my ego and competitive nature at the door. We have all seen many dads live vicariously through their sons, trying to fulfill some childhood dream that never materialized. I am also guilty of that. On more than one occasion I have gotten a little too wrapped up in Micah's peewee soccer game. I have to remind myself this it's about him and not me. It's also not always about winning, although I do think it's important to teach him that someone wins and someone loses at the end of each game.

Finally, patience has never been my strong suit. While I am delighted that he is an athletic little boy, I find myself frequently pushing him to get better. I need to stay mindful that he'll develop on his own schedule, and I am just along for the ride. This dad business is not easy!

How to Give Sports a "Test Run"

If you're not 100 percent sure your child is ready for a team sports commitment, you could try enrolling him or her in a multi-sports class. These are often free and available down to age three. This type of class enables little ones to try out soccer, hockey, T-ball, track-and-field games and other sports to see what they might enjoy most. And while they're giving it a test run, they're running off some of that energy that drives you crazy at home. We put Micah in a multi-sports class through our local recreation center when he was about four or five years old, and it was a great introduction to sports for him.

If your son or daughter isn't ready to join a team, there are plenty of ways he or she can exercise and have fun. Typically, kids enjoy riding a tricycle or bicycle, skipping rope, playing catch, throwing a Frisbee, learning somersaults and cartwheels, dancing, hiking, playing tag or freeze tag, playing outdoor hide-and-seek or kick the can. In summer, there's playing at the beach or pool and running through the sprinkler; and in winter, sledding and making snow forts. The important thing is to engage in physical activity. The National Association of Sports and Physical Education recommends preschoolers get at least one hour of adult-led physical activity and one hour of free play daily.[2]

Here's another thing to consider if your children are in school already. Please don't think that the 15 to 20 minutes of recess is enough for them; they absolutely need more play time when they get home. Children used to have two 20-minute recesses and an hour and 15 minutes to walk home and back for lunch, according to my mom. Now, many schools are removing all physical activity for our children, and I believe this is partially to blame for the high obesity rate in our country. Kids need to move and be active, not only for their physical wellbeing but for their mental and emotional wellbeing as well.

There is another side to sports that some might not have considered, and that is spiritual development. I don't believe it's right to pray for another team to lose, but it's always good to pray with your child that he or she will show good sportsmanship, be an example of a Christlike spirit and do his or her personal best. You can mention Christian role models who are also sports professionals, such as Tim Tebow, winner of two NCAA National Football Championships. He publicly prays on the field and confesses his love for Christ.

Through sports we can teach our children how to live out Philippians 2:14-15: "Do all things without complaining and disputing, that you may become blameless and harmless, children of God without fault in the midst of a crooked and perverse generation, among whom you shine as lights in the world." What is the Holy Spirit saying to us about being "stars" in this world? Is God looking for the fastest runner, the person who scored the most points or crossed the finish line first? That's not what it says. And come to think of it, I believe there's a message for parents in there too.

Dan and I are both very competitive, but I may be even more so because of my days of competing in the fitness contests. That competitive nature still is very strong in my blood, so I love to see my children do well at their sports; nevertheless, there are many times when I need to step back, close my mouth and let them just enjoy being children without worrying about whether they'll win or lose.

May we, as parents, model good sportsmanship even when we don't agree with the official's call. May we cheer on our child's team without grumbling and arguing. May we show a good sense of humor, without sarcasm, when things don't go our way. May we be gracious winners without boasting or bragging. May we remember to smile at others, especially those on the opposite team. May we encourage, not criticize, the children.

Above all, may we who are sitting in the grandstand, or cheering from the sidelines, be parents who shine like stars for Jesus Christ in this world.

Parent's Prayer

Dear Lord,

Thank You for the opportunity we have to play, engage in sports and join teams. Thank You for so many fun and enjoyable things to do on earth.

Give me the wisdom to know when my child is ready to join a sports team, and help us find the one that is right for him or her. Proverbs 3:5-6 tells us to acknowledge You in all our ways and You will direct our paths. So I am claiming that Scripture now for my family.

Help me to teach my child good sportsmanship and to model it as well. Give me the grace and patience not to display ungodly anger or to grumble and complain against the coaches, captains or other officials, because I don't want my child to grow up thinking that is okay. Let every member of our family be a shining light in this dark world. Let us display a loving and Christlike spirit, both to teammates and to the opposing teams.

And, Lord, please protect my child from injury or harm in all he or she does.

In Jesus' name, amen.

Scriptures for Thought and Meditation

In all these things we are more than conquerors through Him who loved us.
ROMANS 8:37

Love is patient, love is kind. It does not envy, it does not boast, it is not proud. It does not dishonor others, it is not self-seeking, it is not easily angered, it keeps no record of wrongs.
1 CORINTHIANS 13:4-5, NIV

My Journal

Your first individual sports or activities:

_____
_____
_____
_____
_____
_____
_____

_____
_____
_____
_____
_____
_____
_____
_____

Your first team sports:

_____
_____
_____
_____
_____
_____
_____
_____
_____
_____
_____
_____
_____
_____
_____
_____

Notes
1. Amanda Rock, "Are Kids' Sports Good for Preschoolers?" http://preschoolers.about.com/od/activitiesfun/f/kidssports.htm (accessed January 2012).
2. Mary L. Gavin, M.D., reviewer "Should Your Preschoolers Play Sports?" July 2011. http://kidshealth.org/parent/growth/learning/preschool_sports.html, (accessed January 2012).

20

Teaching Kids About Money

Now that Micah is four, soon to be five, he's beginning to realize the value of money. We were at a garage sale yesterday, and he had his little wallet with him to buy something special. I've been teaching him about the values associated with each coin and dollar so he can help count out his money if he sees something he likes. He found a baseball glove and snowboard for only $1 each! So we sat down on the grass and counted out a dollar bill and three quarters, two dimes and a nickel. He paid the lady, which she thought was so cute, and he picked up his great deals. He was so proud that he was able to do almost all of the transaction by himself and that he'd earned his own money by doing extra chores that month.

Kids know a lot about money . . . or at least they think they do. Malia is growing up so quickly. The other day she suggested that I just "use my credit card" when I told her I didn't have enough money for the princess skirt she wanted. She's only three now and is obviously not old enough to comprehend the value of money, but by the age of five, most children can begin to learn about earning, budgeting, spending, saving and giving. When children grow up with the right concepts and perspectives on money, they have a much better chance of avoiding financial mistakes when they're older. Then (hopefully) they won't use a credit card for an adult version of a princess skirt they can't afford.

A good way to start the education about money is to lay out each type of coin and some paper money. Let your child see and touch the money as you explain the value of each.

When Micah was four, I actually taped the coins onto a piece of construction paper because he was so interested in learning. I wrote the name and value next to each coin so that he could see it and read it. I then explained that toys, clothes, food and most everything else costs money, and that is why grown-ups work hard to earn money. If your child shows an interest, he's ready to learn more.

At some point, your son (or daughter) will probably ask how much money you make. A good answer is something like, "I make just enough to take good care of you." Or, "Adults keep their incomes private, but I will tell you what the minimum wage is in our state." (You would concurrently explain minimum wage.) If you reveal your annual income to your youngster, he or she is likely to spread the news to his friends; so be mindful of how much information you want to make public.

Another good topic to discuss is how to shop and compare to get the best price. I really love getting a good deal, and in these economic times, who doesn't want to be thrifty and economical? I like taking my kids to a toy store to see all the fun toys, but I really love going to garage sales or our local thrift store to find those same toys for a fraction of the price. The Internet-accessed Craigslist is another favorite of ours.

Your next discussion with your children might be about the price of certain items and why stores cannot give away their goods for free. The natural segue to this is the concept of budgeting and saving. While you wouldn't show a young child the complexities of your family budget, now is the right time for him or her to learn that some things that we want are expensive and require waiting for in order to save the money to purchase them.

The concept of delayed gratification is so contradictory to the message our media constantly sends out to buy more, buy now. Yet it's such an important lesson to teach our children. It goes hand in hand with teaching the importance of impulse control, willpower and self-control. Scripture tells us, "A man without self-control is like a city broken into and left without walls" (Prov. 25:28, *ESV*).

The Famous Marshmallow Experiment

A group of 653 four-year-olds were the subject of an experiment conducted by Professor Walter Mischel at Stanford University. Each child was given one marshmallow with this promise: If they saved the marshmallow for 15 minutes while the professor left the room, they would then be given a second marshmallow upon his return. Some children ate their marshmallow right away, unable to wait. Others stared at the marshmallow longingly; one child even stroked the marshmallow, and some distracted themselves by seeking out a toy to play with. Those children managed to hold off in order to double their treat.

Over a decade later, Mischel followed up on the subjects. The startling results showed that those children who exercised self-control in saving their marshmallow at age four were more well adjusted psychologically and were more dependable persons. And they scored, on average, 210 points higher on the collegiate Scholastic Aptitude Test. On the other hand, the children who were not able to resist the marshmallow temptation grew up to be adults who struggled in stressful situations, often had trouble paying attention and found it difficult to maintain friendships.[1]

How do you think your child would do on such a test? More importantly, how can you help your child develop willpower and self-control? Jesus said, "One who is faithful in a very little is also faithful in much" (Luke 16:10, *ESV*). If we can help our children to be faithful with small rewards and little amounts of money while they are young, they will be faithful in more important things when they grow up. Our spiritual, emotional, mental and physical sides all work together to determine who we are and what we become. It is an awesome responsibility to shape the character of our sons and daughters; one way to do that is by giving them learning experiences involving money.

Commissions and Allowances for Kids

I believe in giving kids a weekly allowance, or a "commission," as we call it in our family. They earn money for doing *extra work*. Children need to have some chores and responsibilities assigned to them not for pay but because they are part of the family, and all members of a family carry their fair share of the workload. Then there are *extra* tasks they can perform to earn money.

Easy tasks that don't take much time earn a little money, and more difficult, time-consuming tasks earn more money. It's a good idea to post a chart showing their expected, unpaid chores, as well as extra jobs (with the appropriate pay amounts assigned). In chapter 9, I talked about some of the chores my kids do. If Micah wants to earn cash to buy more Lego toys on Craigslist.com, he helps me do additional jobs to earn spending money.

This system teaches responsibility and a good work ethic. I don't believe we should pay our kids for everything they do, because that's not the way life works. But they should be given incentive opportunities to develop the habit of taking the initiative and setting goals. They'll also experience the satisfaction of achievement. Handing children everything they want does not help them grow into strong teens and adults.

As a child growing up in Hawaii, with six siblings, we rarely got anything new. My parents couldn't afford much, and I, being the second girl in the family, usually received hand-me-downs from my sister. When I wanted brand-new clothes, I worked to earn the money myself. I didn't love that as a young teen, but it taught me the value of hard work.

A hands-on method for teaching your kids about handling money is to give them three envelopes labeled "savings," "giving" and "spending." Let them choose how and where to use each one; and remember that this is setting a foundation for later in life.

There are times when your child will make a mistake with his or her money—and that's okay. Mistakes serve as powerful learning experiences. Discuss the situation in a calm, logical manner. Let your child know that everyone makes mistakes, and that is how we learn. It's better to let them make minor mistakes now than to suffer a major loss in their finances and credit status later.

Daddy's Blog

Neither Jen nor I were taught how to handle money when we were young. So after we got married, we were like a lot of young couples, and we made financial errors. We bought a house that was too expensive and made some bad business decisions. That was a tough way to learn. So now we are determined to teach our children sound financial principles so they won't have to go through what we did.

My wife quit working outside the home when Micah was born, and I've been the sole income provider. There have been months when our bills were due in two days and we didn't know what we were going to do.

During those times, we turned to God in prayer and He always provided for us, either by giving me a house sale or a speaking engagement. Now we try to live as debt free as possible and only buy things when we have the cash on hand.

Explaining Debit and Credit

When you're out shopping and use your debit card, you can tell your kids, "This is a bank card. We'll talk about it at home." Later, you can give a simple explanation, such as: "The bank card is like a permission note. It gives the store permission to take money out of my bank account. It's like you giving your sister a note that says she can take money out of your spending envelope (or piggy bank). But the store can only take out the exact price of what I bought. So it's the same as paying with cash. I can pay $10 or I can give them my bankcard and let them take $10 out of my bank account. It ends up being the same."

The concept of a credit card is more advanced and usually discussed at an older age; but if you happen to have an inquisitive child, you can offer a simple explanation, such as: "A credit card keeps track of how much I owe to each store. Then at the end of the month, the credit card company sends me a bill to pay."

As your children grow, you can give more complete answers so that, by the time they're 16, they're well aware of how the credit system works and they know the importance of staying out of debt and paying all contractual promises on time and in full. At that point, you'll want your kids to understand this Scripture: "The borrower is the slave of the lender" (Prov. 22:7). We must live within our means so that we don't become a slave to creditors.

If you didn't have the advantage of growing up with a good financial education, and you find yourself in need of credit improvement, my co-author, Carolyn Warren, offers detailed information on credit scoring and credit repair at www.MortgageHelper.com. (Click on Credit Scoring.)

Giving and Sharing

We read in Deuteronomy 16:17, "Every man shall give as he is able, according to the blessing of the Lord your God which He has given you." Four- and five-year-olds understand the concept of sharing and giving, so you can expand those concepts to their personal money as well.

As soon as my children receive money from their grandparents for a birthday or holiday, they ask me how much they should give to God. It makes me happy to see their eagerness to share. I then try to explain what 10 percent is of the amount they were given.

Sometimes they decide to give it to a charity or take it right to Sunday School. I let them make that choice.

We sit down each month as a family and look at what money God has blessed us with for that month. We have about 10 to 20 ministries we love to support, such as Campus Crusade for Christ, Samaritan's Purse, Compassion International, World Vision, Food for the Poor, Christian Broadcasting Network, Christian and Missionary Alliance, Trinity Broadcasting Network, and Catholic Medical Mission Board. They all rank in the top 100 Christian Charities.[2]

Other favorites are the Option Ultrasound™ Program from Focus on the Family, The 700 Club, the Salvation Army, and Operation Blessing. There are many worthy charities; however, I do encourage you to check out each organization in order to ensure that your money is going to help those in need rather than toward administrative costs and legal fees. To learn what percentage of your charitable contribution goes to the actual need versus administrative, marketing, legal and other costs, go to www.charitynavigator.org.

I want my children to understand where our donation money is going, so I show them pictures or videos on the Internet of the charity we have selected. When they see a video about a family in Africa that must walk half a day to get water each and every day, and they understand their money will go toward a fresh-water pump in their village, they get really excited about giving.

Each Christmas now, for the past 11 years, Dan and I have given bags full of toiletries, food, coats, warm clothes or gift cards to the homeless people in downtown Denver. The first couple of years, we were able to pass out only a few bags. But by the fifth year, we invited our personal training clients and our friends to participate. Last year, we had more than 80 bags and gift cards to deliver to people in need. We take the kids along so they can see how much God has blessed us and how rewarding it is to give to others.

Jesus speaks to us about giving to the poor in Matthew 25:31-46. He said that when we give food, beverage, clothes or shelter to the "least" of society, He counts it as if we are helping Him. As parents, that's easy to understand. If someone does a favor for our little one, it's as though they've done a favor for us personally.

Parent's Prayer

Dear Heavenly Father,

Thank You for the provisions You have given my family. May "Your Kingdom come, Your will be done," and may we continue to have our "daily bread," as promised in the Lord's Prayer.

I ask Your blessing on my employment. I trust You to provide the job opportunities and promotions we need and that are in Your will. Give me sufficient finances to take good care of my family. Help me to use my money in a godly way, showing generosity to those in need, and never being greedy or selfish. Give me the wisdom and self-control to live within my means, avoiding bad debt that becomes an entrapment. Help me use my finances wisely and to live debt free.

Give me a generous heart to give to the ministry and to the poor. I ask for wisdom to know where and when to give. Let my tithes and offerings be as unto You, Lord Jesus.

Please use me to teach my children proper concepts and perspectives about money. I want to guide them to make wise choices and to help them develop a generous spirit. Give me wisdom on how to handle situations that come up.

Lord Jesus, I dedicate all I have to You, for You are the one who bought me with a great price. I give You my talents, my time and my finances. Help me to use every part of my life for Your glory and to further Your kingdom.

In Jesus' name, amen.

Scriptures for Thought and Meditation

He who tills his land will be satisfied with bread, but he who follows frivolity is devoid of understanding.
PROVERBS 12:11

What will it profit a man if he gains the whole world, and loses his own soul?
MARK 8:36

My Journal

Your first allowance or commission was $_____, and it was for:

_____

_____

_____

_____

_____

_____

_____

_____

_____

_____

You were a natural saver or spender. (Circle one.) You spent your money on/you gave your money to:

_____

_____

_____

_____

_____

_____

_____

_____

_____

_____

_____

_____

_____

Notes

1. Jonah Lehrer, "Don't: The Secret of Self-Control," The New Yorker, May 18, 2009. http://www.newyorker.com/reporting/2009/05/18/090518fa_fact_lehrer. (accessed January 2012).
2. For more information, see http://www.christianpost.com/news/christian-charities-rank-high-in-top-100-u-s-nonprofits-30411/.

21

Childhood Fears

Jennifer's Journal

We just got back from Hawaii from a visit to see my parents, and now Malia is afraid of the dark. She insists on sleeping with her light on. It's not like her. Before we left, she was never afraid of the dark. In fact, it was Micah who never wanted to go upstairs by himself after the sun set. And Malia would always pipe up and say, "Micah, I can go upstairs with you. I'm not scared of the dark." It was so cute. And then the two of them would march off together with Malia holding Micah's hand, leading the way. I'm not sure what happened exactly. Maybe it's because we've been gone for a while.

Lord, please give my children courage in this scary world. Help them to be brave, and help me to teach them Your Word, Lord, because it says that the spoken Word of God is alive and powerful, like a double-edged sword in our mouths (see Heb. 4:12). Your Word can give us power over our fears.

Don't be surprised if your three-, four- or five-year-old suddenly begins to experience feelings of fear. Sorting through fear is a natural part of growing up. Some fear is necessary for survival, as is pain. If we never felt fear or pain, most of us wouldn't live very long. As parents, we get to teach our kids which fears are valid, and which are invalid or to be dismissed. The dismissed fears then cease to exist.

At the toddler and preschool age, children have not fully grasped cause-and-effect. Neither do they have a clear distinction between reality and fantasy. When we guide them through the thought process, they learn which fears are safe to eliminate. For example, young children might see a scary animal in the corner of their room at night and cry out; but when we come and turn on the light, they see it's only a pile of clothes. By using a calm voice and turning the light off and on, we can show them there is nothing to be afraid of. One little boy saw scary shapes on his wall at night and was afraid. But when his dad came into the room and showed him it was only the reflection of the tree branches outside his window, his fear went away.

When you are dealing with your child's fearfulness, never belittle or poke fun at him or her. Parents are to be their children's defenders and protectors, not their accusers. It's one thing to laugh *with* your child at the "funny clothes monster," but it's something altogether different to ridicule the child. For many months, Micah did not like to sleep with his closet doors open. Each night after I prayed for him and kissed him goodnight, I'd be walking out and then hear, "Mom, can you please close my closet doors?" I always did and reassured him, but it took awhile for him to get over the fear of something bad in his closet.

"Social referencing" is a term used when children look to their parents to see what type of emotional response they should experience in a situation. We've all seen a child fall and get a scraped knee, then look at mommy to see whether or not it's serious. If mom looks horrified, he'll burst out bawling; but if mom stays calm, he probably won't even cry, or won't cry much. Social referencing is especially important to understand when it comes to fear. We literally teach our kids whether or not to fear a spider, a glass elevator or a dark room by how we react.

As I mentioned earlier, some fear is healthy. We want our children to fear touching a hot stove, running out into traffic or inserting a metal object into an electrical outlet. But we don't want them growing up to fear all those things we wish we weren't afraid of ourselves. By being careful how we react, we can protect our children from developing unnecessary fears.

With my firstborn, Micah, my motherly instinct was to protect him from all harm. Whenever he'd get hurt, I'd run over to see if he was okay. I made too big of a deal about it. With Malia, well, let's just say she's one tough cookie. When she fell down and scraped her knee, she barely thought twice about it because I didn't make a big deal about it. I think that by the second child and beyond, you realize that your children will get hurt but they are resilient. It's always the right thing to pray over our children and ask God to cover them with His protection and put His angels around them. And then we trust that He is always good and knows best even when we experience all that life can bring in a fallen world.

One of the wonderful things about raising children is that it challenges us to become better people and to develop emotionally and spiritually ourselves. When my children arrived, it absolutely changed and challenged me spiritually. I questioned the old CDs I used to listen to, the clothes I used to wear that still hung in my closet, and the words that came out of my mouth when I was angry. I vowed to change my ways and become a better person for them. I try to remember to pray each night that God will help me become a better mom than I was the day before.

Daddy's Blog

From birth to age five, I lived in Liverpool, New York, a suburb of Syracuse. I loved that old colonial home more than I can describe. Before my parents got divorced, we lived there with my sister and brother. Michael was 10 years older than me, and from my mother's first marriage; but he was a true-blue brother in every sense of the word.

There was a long, dark hallway that led to the stairs going up to my second-floor bedroom. On each side of the stairs was a doorway. The doorway on the right led to the formal living room, and the doorway to the left led to the formal dining room.

One night, on my way up to my room, Michael hid behind the wall of the doorway leading into the living room. As I started up the stairs, Michael jumped out from behind the wall with a loud yell. That scared the tar right out of me, and I tore up those stairs so fast I burned the carpet. I never forgot that, and I was scared to go upstairs by myself every day I lived in that house.

Early on, my son, Micah, wanted to play hide-and-seek. He seemed to really like it when I would hide and then pop out and scare him. As he got older, he didn't like it much anymore. I am not sure what changed, but we don't play hide-and-seek anymore. Sometimes I forget and do the macho thing, telling Micah, "Go downstairs, there's nothing to be afraid of." But then I remember my brother Michael jumping out at me, and I realize I need to respect and affirm Micah's feelings.

Your Fears Are Not You

Fear is not a personality trait, and we don't have to accept it into our lives. I've always been encouraged when I read 2 Timothy 1:7, which puts fear in its proper place and helps me focus on what I have because of God's presence in my life: "For God has not given us a spirit of fear, but of power and of love and of a sound mind."

Recently, I noticed Micah struggling with fear, or the lack of courage, so we stopped in at Inklings, the Christian bookstore in our church, and I picked out a shield necklace for him to wear over his heart. The shield has these words inscribed on it:

Be strong and courageous. Do not be terrified; do not be discouraged, for the LORD your God will be with you wherever you go (Josh. 1:9, *NIV*).

When he's feeling scared or insecure, he can touch his shield to be reminded that he is not alone.

When fear comes, God's Word tells us what to do: "Whenever I am afraid, I will trust in you" (Ps. 56:3). And then verse 4 says, "In God I have put my trust; I will not fear." Those two verses show the progression of (1) feeling fear, (2) putting your trust in God, and (3) getting rid of fear. That is the process for handling fear, and we can teach it to our children so that they grow up to be courageous.

What if you have longstanding phobias? Then you can claim Psalm 34:4: "I sought the LORD, and He heard me, and delivered me from all my fears." This promise is for you and your entire family. (Even if you seek professional help for a phobia, you can take Psalm 34:4 in your heart with you.) Again, "God has not given us a spirit of fear, but of power and of love and of a sound mind" (2 Tim. 1:7).

Unholy Spirits

Ephesians 6:10-20 tells us that we are in a spiritual warfare, fighting against the schemes of Satan.

Jesus, when He was here on earth, cast out demons as He ministered among the people. We read of one such situation in Luke 9:37-43, where Jesus freed a man's son from a demonic spirit.

Acts 5:16 tells about Peter healing the sick and those who were tormented by unclean spirits. These and other accounts let us know that there are fallen angels, commonly called unclean, unholy or demonic spirits, on the earth. If your child experiences an unusual and severe fear that is above and beyond one of the natural childhood fears most families work through, it would be appropriate to spend time in prayer, asking God to reveal to you what it is.

When Micah was five, he suddenly woke up with night terrors. It was much more than being afraid of the dark or having a bad dream. He'd look in a certain direction in his room and describe a monstrous figure he saw. The expression on his face was one of indescribable terror. Dan and I would hold our son and pray with him until it went away and he fell back asleep. It usually took about 15 minutes.

This kept happening, night after night, but he did not remember these occurrences the next morning. Nevertheless, they continued to happen about three to four nights a week for months. At first we didn't know what to do. Then I reread *The Power of a Praying Parent* by Stormie Omartian, in which she said something similar happened at their house, and God revealed to her that they needed to get rid of an action adventure video game that was in her son's room—one that he had borrowed from a friend. She removed the game and she and her husband anointed his room with oil as described in Exodus 40:9. As soon as they did that, the nightmares stopped immediately.

I prayed and asked God to show me what was causing these horrible night visions our son was having. And God was faithful to answer that prayer. He led me to find two books my children had received as gifts, and one toy that was offensive, in Micah's room.

I hadn't paid much attention to the books, because they were written for older children; in fact, we hadn't even read them yet. But as I looked through the pages, I saw that they were inappropriate. I don't know what type of religion or witchcraft the author might have been involved in, but those books and the toy had to go. I threw them out immediately and then I prayed through his room for all evil to be gone and for the presence of the Holy Spirit to bring peace. I anointed his room with oil, and from that time on, Micah has never had another nighttime terror.

My children know that we all have authority over evil in the name of Jesus Christ, our Savior. We are told in Scripture, "For this purpose the Son of God [Jesus] was manifested, that He might destroy the works of the devil" (1 John 3:8). Even the basic Lord's Prayer says, "Deliver us from the evil one" (Matt. 6: 13). We are not to fear that which is unholy or evil; but rather, we are to be victorious through the power and name of Jesus.

It is important that we do not invite evil into our homes or into our children's lives through frightening so-called children's movies or horror shows on television. It is our duty as parents to protect our children from evil. When I hear about some of the shows parents allow to come in through their TV sets, it is no wonder their children have nightmares. And don't believe you can have violence, bloody images and soft porn on your television without your children noticing. Even if they're playing in the other room, they know. I exhort you to shut off those channels and spend the time doing something uplifting, such as reading a *good* book, playing a board game, doing an art project, learning to play an instrument or any one of a number of fun activities.

My husband has made Bible reading a nightly family activity. We started with Genesis at the beginning of the year, and we are steadily making our way through the Bible. Sure, there are evenings when we are out to dinner and don't get the reading in; but if we're home, and we forget, one of the kids is quick to remind us, "We didn't read our Bible tonight."

After Dan finishes his Bible reading, both of our children have their own children's Bible or devotionals to read as well. Some of their favorites are Sheila Walsh's *God's Little Princess Devotional Bible: Bible Storybook* and *God's Mighty Warrior Devotional Bible.* They also enjoy *Jesus Calling: 365 Devotions for Kids* by Sarah Young; and *The Beginner's Bible: Timeless Children's Stories* by various authors and Kelly Pulley. When they finish one, they move on to the next; and now that Micah can read, he is in charge of reading his own chapter each night. We want him to get into the habit of reading his Bible to himself each and every day.

As the promises of God's Word get into our children's hearts and minds, many of the fears they used to have simply have faded away.

Parent's Prayer

Dear Lord,

We know that fear does not come from You, but from the evil one. When we follow You, Jesus, Your Word says we have nothing to fear, because You are with us. Help us use Your authority by speaking Your truths when situations arrive, such as when our children have nightmares or night terrors. Please help me teach my children that they also can speak Your mighty name, and fear must flee.

Jennifer Polimino & Carolyn Warren

I love Your promise of help when we trust You: "All you who fear the LORD, trust the LORD! He is your helper and your shield" (Ps. 115:11, NLT). Heavenly Father, please place Your shield over my children right now. Protect them from all evil and keep them safe.

I pray that no harm will ever come to my child, and I thank You in advance for watching over him/her. I also ask You to help me keep trusting You in a fallen world. You are always loving and always good, no matter what happens.

And, Lord, please help me to be a better mom/dad tomorrow than I was today.

In Your mighty name I pray, amen.

Scriptures for Thought and Meditation

Have I not commanded you? Be strong and of good courage; do not be afraid; nor be dismayed, for the Lord your God is with you wherever you go.
JOSHUA 1:9

Do not tremble; do not be afraid. Did I not proclaim my purposes for you long ago? You are my witnesses—is there any other God? No! There is no other Rock—not one!
ISAIAH 44:8, NLT

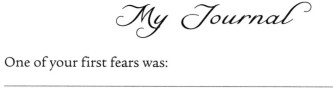

One of your first fears was:

_____

_____

_____

_____

_____

_____

_____

_____
_____
_____
_____
_____
_____

How we worked through that fear:

_____
_____
_____
_____
_____
_____
_____
_____
_____
_____
_____
_____
_____

This is my favorite Scripture on fear, which we prayed over you:

_____
_____
_____
_____
_____
_____
_____
_____
_____
_____
_____
_____

22

Leading Your Child to Jesus

Jennifer's Journal

I thought the day my children were born would be the most important day of their lives. Now I realize the most important day for them will be the day they accept Jesus into their hearts as their personal Lord and Savior.

Micah is at the age where we've been talking a lot about salvation. He's been asking many questions about heaven and where he will go when he dies, since we returned from attending the memorial service for a dear friend. I've been explaining to him that as humans, we have all sinned and that the only way into heaven is to ask God to forgive our sins and to believe that Jesus is the Son of God. I explained that he needs to ask Jesus into his heart, and then he will know for sure that he will get to spend eternity in heaven with Jesus.

Dan was out of town, and the kids and I were sitting in the kitchen reading our nightly Bible study. Micah ran upstairs to get something, and when he returned he had a cute little smile on his face. "I'm ready to say 'the prayer', Mommy," he said.

"Really?" I asked. I was so excited since we'd been talking about it for weeks now! I was holding Malia in my lap, and I reached over and took his sweet little hand in mine. I asked him a few questions to make sure he understood, and then I told him he was ready to repeat these words after me. And right there in our kitchen, he gave his life to Jesus Christ. What a special, joyful day it was—the most important day of his life!

When your child reaches the age when he or she is ready to ask Jesus into his (or her) heart, this is the beginning of a journey of faith that will last a lifetime. I believe that as parents, the most important thing we can teach our children is that Jesus is the Son of God, He came to save us, He loves us and He forgives us of all our sins when we pray and believe in His name (when we believe that He paid for our sins on the cross and won the victory over death, which is our inheritance as well when we believe in Him).

Nana's Journal

Last week, my elementary-age granddaughters went to the nursery class to lead the toddlers in worship. They did Bible action songs, such as "Deep and Wide," "Climb Up Sunshine Mountain" and "Jesus Loves Me." These girls love the Lord, and they love to worship.

I was not yet in kindergarten when I prayed at the altar with my father when our pastor invited the congregation to come and seek the Lord after the sermon. The presence of God was there. As I told Jesus I loved Him, my heart was so filled with His love for me that I was moved to tears of joy. This happened week after week.

"God is giving you a blessing," my father explained.

There is no doubt that little ones can know Jesus and experience His wonderful love.

Carolyn Warren

Talking with Your Child About Salvation

Before you pray the salvation prayer with your child, you need to lay a foundation. Talk about Jesus, who He is, and why He came to earth. Tell the stories about Jesus, about how He loves us, how everywhere He went He cared for people and did good things for them. Jesus healed the sick, raised the dead, fed the hungry multitude and had complete authority over nature, as demonstrated when He calmed the storm when His disciples were afraid in the boat. Your local Christian bookstore will have storybooks and children's Bibles with colorful illustrations to help you tell the truth of the gospel.

In addition, lay the foundation of their understanding with prayer. Pray that God will reveal His great and wonderful love to your son (or daughter). And pray that He will make you aware of the right time to lead your child to Jesus.

You can also share your own story about how you asked Jesus into your heart, and how He came in and took away your sins, made you feel clean inside and filled your heart with His love. As you probably know, kids love to hear stories about their parents, and your own testimony is a powerful tool for the Holy Spirit to use.

Be sensitive to your child's spiritual readiness. God loves the little ones, and there is no need to push before they are mature enough to understand. I made a mistake here early on.

Over a year ago, I was so excited for Micah to "say the prayer" with me that I led him through it before he was able to totally understand. Later, when he told me he was ready, we prayed the salvation prayer together again while we were sitting in the kitchen. This time he understood, and it was a very real and sweet experience.

As the parent, you know your child better than anybody, so you'll know when your son or daughter has reached that level of maturity and understanding. You might also ask questions to confirm it. For example, here are the type of questions I asked Micah:

- "Micah, do you know what sin is?" (*Sin is disobeying God.*)

- "Do you know how many people in the world have sinned?" (*"For all have sinned and fall short of the glory of God"* [Rom. 3:23].)

- "Do you understand what God's punishment is for sin?" (*"For the wages of sin is death, but the gift of God is eternal life in Christ Jesus our Lord"* [Rom. 6:23].)

- "Do you know who the Lord Jesus is?" (*The Son of God and our Savior.*)

- "Do you understand why Jesus died on the cross?" (*To pay the penalty for our sins so that we could be forgiven.*)

- "Do you know why you need Jesus as your Savior?" (*"Because I have sinned or disobeyed." If your child says no, simply say, Jesus loves you, and we'll talk more about it another time. You can continue telling stories of the goodness of Jesus as your child matures.*)

- "Are you ready to ask Jesus to forgive you and to come into your heart? And are you ready to live for Him every day?" (*If your child says no, that's okay. Again, give him or her more time to grow into understanding what it's all about.*)

Don't feel bad if your child isn't ready the first time you ask. It's better to wait until they're old enough to understand and will have a more meaningful experience.

Years earlier, Micah had memorized John 3:16, "For God so loved the world that He gave His only begotten Son, that whosoever believes in Him should not perish but have everlasting life." Even though Micah recited the words, he didn't understand the significance of this verse at that time, since he was only two years old at the time.

However, when your son or daughter tells you he (or she) is ready, don't make him (or her) wait. Jesus said, "Let the little children come to Me, and do not forbid them; for of such is the kingdom of God" (Luke 18:16). Our senior pastor, Dr. Jim Dixon, recently shared with our congregation how his mother led him to Jesus when he was just five years old:

We were living in California, and I was about four years old when I began talking with my mother about going to heaven. Even at that young age, I understood disobedience and was feeling insecure about my eternal life. As the months passed, my mother told me about Jesus' love, how He died on the cross for our sins and how we need to turn our lives over to Him. My mom was really the evangelizer in our home for my brothers and me.

After turning five, one day I knelt beside her in our living room. With our knees on the carpet, our elbows on the sofa and hands folded, I asked the Lord Jesus to come into my heart and forgive me of my sins. I asked Him to wash me whiter than snow. The presence of the Lord was with us, and as I ended the prayer with "from this day forth, I will seek to follow Him," I was tearing up. That was 61 years ago!

What an encouraging story from a man who now leads more than 6,000 members to follow Christ at Cherry Hills Church in Highlands Ranch, Colorado!

Leading Your Child Through the Salvation Prayer

For young children, I believe that guiding them through the prayer is most helpful. Here is a sample salvation prayer that is simple enough for a child. It includes three elements: (1) confession, (2) repentance, and (3) acknowledgment.

Dear Lord Jesus, I have disobeyed and sinned. I am sorry for my sins. Please forgive me and come into my heart. Jesus, I believe You are God's Son and You are my Lord and Savior. I give my life to You now. Thank You, Jesus. Amen.

After praying, it's a good idea to ask a couple questions to make sure your child has understood.

- "Where is Jesus now?" (*Your child might say, "In my heart," or "He is with me."*)
- "Do you know Jesus has forgiven your sins and that you are going to heaven?" (*Yes.*)

This is a good time to teach your precious child God's wonderful promise in Hebrews 13:5: "I will never leave you." I taught Micah to put his name in place of "you." He has memorized it as, "Never will I leave Micah." Personalizing a condition or promise verse should help your children understand the commitment between them and God.

After Micah had prayed the salvation prayer, I gave him a big hug. This is a celebration! Luke 15:7 says there is a lot of rejoicing in heaven when someone comes into salvation. I never wanted my son to forget this special day. So, I quickly got out my camera and took a picture of him. Then I told him we were going to pick out something very special to remember this day. After school the following day, we stopped by our church bookstore, Inklings, and got him a brand-new "big boy" *Kids Quest Study Bible.* I took a picture of him holding it. On the flyleaf I wrote the date that he accepted Jesus as his Savior so that he wouldn't forget or ever question whether or not he had been saved.

I also explained to Micah that his name is now written in God's Book of Life (see Rev. 3:5). If he meant the prayer that he prayed, then his name is in God's book *forever.* This is so special! The angels in heaven sing and praise God about a new name—Micah's name—being written in God's book. Scripture promises, "To all who believed him and accepted him, he gave the right to become children of God" (John 1:12, *NLT*).

When I think back about that special time, I almost get tears in my eyes. There is no greater joy as a parent than seeing your children love and serve our wonderful Lord. I'm looking forward to the time when Malia is old enough to make this same commitment.

We pray *through* our child's years from birth to age five and beyond. But in addition, we also pray *with* them. Praise the name of Jesus forever!

Parent's Prayer

Dear Father,

I come to You today with thanksgiving in my heart that You sent Your Son to die on the cross so that we might be saved. Jesus, thank You that You came to earth for me and for my child. You paid the penalty for sin and died a sinner's death, when You were sinless, so that we might live in eternity with You.

Please help me to properly lead my children to You. Teach me to be the example that You want me to be. Help me to know when my child is ready to accept You into his/her heart; and help me to present Your message clearly.

I believe that heaven is a real place, and it's where I want to live forever with You, Lord. I need Your guidance to be able to talk to my children about heaven so that the desire to live there grows in their hearts more and more each day.

When they are feeling down or hurting inside, let them know that this is temporary and that in heaven there is no sadness, no sickness and no pain. I claim Revelation 21:4: "God will wipe away every tear from their eyes; there shall be no more death, nor sorrow, nor crying. There shall be no more pain, for the former things have passed away."

Lord, we can't wait to feel that comfort and be with You in paradise for eternity. You say this earth is not our home, and we believe what it says in Your Word. Thank You, Jesus, for loving us so very much.

In Your heavenly name we pray, amen.

Scriptures for Thought and Meditation

When someone becomes a Christian he becomes a brand new
person inside. He is not the same any more. A new life has begun!
2 CORINTHIANS 2:17, TLB

The LORD is my strength and my song; and He has become my salvation;
He is my God, and I will praise Him; my father's God, and I will exalt him.
EXODUS 15:2

My Journal

As a keepsake, write your remembrance of your child's salvation experience here:

_____

_____

_____

_____

_____

_____

_____

_____

_____

_____

_____

_____

_____

_____

_____

_____

_____

_____

_____

23

Jennifer's Testimony

Jennifer's Journal

I hid my former life for years, never wanting any of my new Christian friends or clients to know all the horrible things that I did in my past. The guilt was overwhelming me and was at times just suffocating. I remember many days and nights crying out to God to take away the guilt, pain and jealousy that I felt. There were days when I just wanted to die, so ashamed of what I had done. Did I even deserve to live?

When I was pregnant for the first time, I was lying in bed alone one night. Dan and I had had another fight about my insecurities, and I ran upstairs. I just lay there with tears streaming down my face. I cried and cried out to Jesus. And this time, He came to me! I had never had an encounter with Him before, but this time I fully felt the presence of God in my room. I was no longer alone. I felt Him hold me and tell me of the love He had for me, and how I was going to make a great mother. In that moment, I was at complete peace. I had never felt such love and reassurance before.

I didn't completely understand this meeting with Jesus until I read the introduction of a book called Jesus Calling. *The author, Sarah Young, talks about her visitations from Jesus as well. I was in awe that I had had a similar experience. It has never happened to me again, although I invite Him to grace me with His presence at any time.*

When I was three years old, my parents decided they wanted to raise their family in a better place than Chicago, so they loaded up our motor home, their three kids and headed out for a three-and-a-half-month trip across the continental United States. We ventured into 43 states; but as we drew near the end of summer, my parents were convinced they were still in search of their dream home.

A few weeks later, we embarked on another journey, this time across the South Pacific. Over the next three-and-a-half months, we flew on 24 different flights. My parents took us to five islands in French Polynesia, as well as Samoa, Fiji and Hawaii. They absolutely fell in love with the Hawaiian islands. We flew back to Chicago where my parents sold their antique collection and other assets. Eventually, they chose a small town on the Big Island of Hawaii called Kailua-Kona. It was 1974, and I was four-and-a-half years old when we packed up and moved to this tiny town that didn't even have one traffic light in it!

Soon after the move, my mom was pregnant again, and then again—until we had a total of seven children running around the house. When we weren't in school, we spent our days at the beach swimming, boogie boarding, surfing, catching fish and exploring the tide pools.

I was very blessed to grow up in a Christian home. My mother was a stay-at-home mom, and I have always told people that her greatest gift from God is being an awesome mother. No matter what we put her through, she was always there for us, teaching us about Him, and teaching us right from wrong. And my dad was great too. He worked very hard and encouraged us to always trust in God to provide for all of our needs.

One day, when I was just 12 years old, my life completely changed. I was molested by a group of four boys. I went from being an innocent, young girl to a hurt and confused young women.[1]

I told no one about what had happened to me. When I was 15 years old, I was crying out for help in all the wrong ways. I started drinking and soon began dating. My first real boyfriend was 18. I thought he was so cool, on his way to college. Little did I know he had a bet going with his friends to see how many girls he could "conquer" before he left. I was date raped, and because of the shame I felt at the time, again I told no one.

The following year, I fell hard for a boy I thought was the love of my life. We were together for almost a year, and I got pregnant. I was in the tenth grade. There was no way that we could keep our baby, or so I was told; so I did the unthinkable. At 16, I got an abortion. I cut school, boarded a plane to Honolulu, and was back home before dinner. My parents never even knew a thing. I cried the whole time. I hated myself, and I didn't want to live.

A few weeks later, I walked down our street into an empty subdivision with a razor in my hand. I started to make scratches on my wrists, but someone had told me that if you took your own life, you would go to hell. This belief actually saved my life. But because of the abortion, I vowed never to have children. How could I be a good mother when I had aborted my first child? In my heart, I never wanted to do it, but I was only a scared teenager and felt pressured into this decision. I wish I had been able to speak up and tell someone. If only someone who cared had been at that clinic that day.

I struggled with this for years and years and went to counseling again and again in an attempt to "get over it," but it never seemed to go away.

After graduating from high school, I tried to run away from it all. I went to college in Long Beach, California, but soon I got into the party scene there as well. I was in many unhealthy relationships and truly didn't care if I lived or died.

Right after graduating from college, I jumped on my friend's boat and headed for the South Pacific for my own adventure. We had a wonderful time sailing from American Samoa to Tonga and then on to Fiji. But after five months, I started missing home. It was my mom's birthday, so I decided to surprise her and bought a plane ticket back to Hawaii. It was not a smart move on my part. Within the first week back, I met a guy, and thinking I should do it God's way this time, I married him—after just six months. I didn't really even know him. I divorced this abusive man and proceeded on to the next bad relationship.

By this time, I had started competing in fitness competitions. I won the Ms. Fitness Hawaii, and soon the photographers wanted to take pictures of me. I was thrilled that someone thought I was pretty. Soon they were asking me to do sexy photos that I now wish I hadn't done. But at that point in my life, I was so far away from God, it didn't seem like a big deal to me.

I was so vulnerable and insecure that I would let anyone tell me what to do. I moved to Denver with the latest man in my life, and I continued competing and won the Ms. Fitness Colorado contest. The guy I was dating convinced me to work at a gentleman's club. This was the lowest point in my life. I had absolutely no self-esteem, and I knew I needed to get out of this sinful life I was leading.

God knew that the only way He was going to get my attention was through a man. That's when Dan entered the picture. In September 1999, I met my husband, Dan, at a restaurant in downtown Denver on a girls' night out. We had both been dating, but wanted more. He had just rededicated his life to Jesus. It was providential because just the week before I had made a long list telling God what I needed in a man; being a Christian was number 1 on my list.

We starting dating, and we quickly decided that we wanted this relationship to be according to God's plan. He helped me quit my unhealthy night job and I started going to church with him. We began planning our life together, but we had a long road ahead of us. The men in my past had destroyed so much of me.

Our first year of marriage was very difficult; we almost got divorced. We are both very hardheaded, strong-willed people, and he had his own issues from his past. Soon, life took over and the bills started piling up. We both worked long hours in our personal training business, trying to make it a big success. We were doing it our way and not God's. We listened to the wrong people instead of listening to God. We made the wrong choices, and we found ourselves way over our heads in debt.

During that time, we had entered our fifth year of marriage and had decided that it was about time to have a baby. I had put it off for a long time, but Dan kept asking. My insecurities took over; I was so scared of losing my body that I had worked so hard to get. I thought that being pregnant would mean that I would get fat and that I would be unattractive to my husband. I convinced myself that he'd find someone else, as had previous men in my life. I had been cheated on so many times before.

Most important, I was afraid that I wasn't going to be a good mother. My words "I never deserve to have children" rang in my head throughout each day.

In addition, starting a family would be a strain on us financially, and I did not want a baby unless I could be a stay-at-home mother like my mom was. That would subtract half of our income. In my heart, I knew that God would provide for our needs—and He always has. Although some months have been really tight, God has always proven to us that He is in control.

So we finally started trying, but we just couldn't get pregnant. By the fifth month, we wondered if something was wrong with one of us, so Dan went and got tested—but wouldn't you know it, later that month we found out the good news: I was expecting!

And then something happened when I became pregnant. Even though I was a Christian and had accepted Jesus as my Lord and Savior, I still didn't *know* Him or follow Him like I should. But during my pregnancy, I grew closer to God than ever before. There was never a day that went by when I didn't talk to God and pray for my baby. I told God *everything*—how I felt, how scared I was, and I asked Him to please let me be a good mother. And most important, I prayed for my baby. I prayed for health, joy and wisdom—every day. Each week I researched the baby's development, and I prayed for that specific body part as well. And you know what? God answered every single prayer for my child.

Our sweet baby, Micah Kekoa Polimino, came into this world on August 5, 2005, and I have never been happier in my life. I used to say, "I'm never having kids, no way." Thank the Lord that He had different plans for me and has blessed us beyond measure with this beautiful little soul. I have learned so much about being a mother, and every day, God is teaching me something about Himself through this little boy. He's teaching me about compassion and grace and about unconditional love and trust.

And, as you know, Micah is an older brother. Malia Grace came into our lives on March 19, 2008, and she is as much of a blessing as her brother. I can see that the special prayers that I prayed for her are coming to pass as well. You can read all about how to pray for your unborn baby in my first book, *Praying Through Your Pregnancy.*

As you can see, it doesn't matter what you've done in your past. God is greater than your past. I'm not a perfect mother—far from it—but I do my best; and most importantly, I teach my kids about Jesus, our Lord and Savior. So today, I'm here to encourage you to ask God to forgive you of your past, if you haven't already done so. Pour out your heart to Him and let Him wash you white as snow. God has amazing plans for your life, and the only way to live the life He has planned for you is to walk side by side with Him.

If you have never given your life to Jesus Christ, I invite you to do so now. Or perhaps you want to rededicate your life to the Lord. It's very simple. All you have to do is to acknowledge Jesus as your Lord and Savior, ask Him to forgive you of all wrongdoing and invite Him into your life to be the Savior and Lord of your life.

God loves you no matter what you may have done. John 3:16 says, "For God loved the world so much that he gave his one and only Son, so that everyone who believes in him will not perish but have eternal life" (*NLT*).

God will forgive you and accept you. Romans 10:13 says, "Whoever calls on the name of the Lord shall be saved." I would love it if you would say this prayer with me.

Salvation Prayer

*Dear Jesus, I believe You are the Son of God
and that You died for me on the cross so that I may live
with You in heaven forever. Please forgive me for
my sins and give me the gift of eternal life.
I want You to be part of my life.
Please come into my heart today.
I want to know You and serve You always.
In Your name I pray, Jesus. Amen.*

Parent's Prayer

Dear Heavenly Father,

Thank You for Your grace and Your forgiveness. Thank You for loving me as much as You love my child. I am Your child, God, and I long to hear You say, "with you I am well pleased."

Help me not to look back at my past, but to look ahead at the future; and help me to be the parent You desire me to be. Help me to be more Christlike in my daily walk. When my children look at me, let them see You, Jesus.

Being a parent is, by far, the most difficult yet the most rewarding job. Awaken Your Sprit within me, Jesus, and allow me to look at and love my child through Your eyes, Your love.

Heavenly Father, You are the Creator of all! You are our prime example of how to be a parent, how to love our children and how to disciple them. Tell me how to nurture and guide them, and tell me when to let go and let You take over.

Teach me Your ways, O Lord, and show me the right paths to lead my children to You. Above all else, help me to prepare my children for Your return.

I pray this in Your holy name, Jesus, amen.

Scriptures for Thought and Meditation

He will again have compassion on us, and will
subdue our iniquities. You will cast all
of our sins into the depths of the sea.
MICAH 7:19

Come to Me, all you who labor and are
heavy laden, and I will give you rest. Take My yoke upon you
and learn from Me, for I am gentle and lowly
in heart, and you will find rest for your souls.
For My yoke is easy and My burden is light.
MATTHEW 11:28-30

My Journal

As you feel comfortable, please share your testimony about how
you came to know Jesus as your Savior, for your child to read when
he/she is older:

_____
_____
_____
_____
_____
_____
_____
_____
_____
_____
_____
_____
_____
_____
_____
_____

Note

1. To hear more about my story, please watch my interview on *The 700 Club*: http://www.
cbn.com/700club/features/amazing/AR83_jennifer_polimino.aspx. Or you can listen
to it on Focus on the Family at: http://www.focusonthefamily.com/Radio.aspx?
ID=%7B938AE697-CF6D-434E-9FB3-FD8A117A93B7%7D.

Acknowledgments

Our heartfelt thanks to our agent, John Willig, president of Literary Services, Inc., for his expertise and support of this project.

We appreciate the team at Regal Books who make it possible for our books to get into the hands of readers around the world. Thank you, Steven Lawson, senior editor, for your foresight. Thank you, Rob Williams, for the beautiful cover design. Thank you, Mark Weising, senior managing editor, for getting our book to the printer on time. Thank you, Jackie Medina, for your work in publicity and for praying through your own pregnancy as you worked on our first book, *Praying Through Your Pregnancy*. Thank you, Deena Davis, for your attention to detail in the copyediting. We also thank Bill Greig III, president of Gospel Light/Regal Books, for believing in our message and having the vision for a series, the *Praying Through* books.

Our gratitude to senior pastor Dr. Jim Dixon of Cherry Hills Community Church in Highlands Ranch, Colorado, for sharing his salvation story. We appreciate Katy Cerny, ministry leader from IHOP; Elisa Morgan, president emerita, MOPS International and publisher of *Fullfill*; and Alexandra Kuykendall, mom and lead content editor for MOPS, for their interviews.

From Carolyn Warren: Honor and respect to Pastor Joe Turner of Shorewood Foursquare Church in Seattle, Washington, for his in-depth Bible teaching and prayers.

From Jennifer Polimino: Micah and Malia, this book is for you. We also want to thank our families. We love you all!

Most of all, we thank the Lord Jesus Christ, to whom we give all glory, praise and honor.

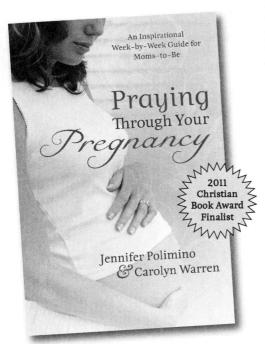